Zazzy Dot

presents

A Puzzle Adventure Around the World

Activity Book for Explorers

wide eyed wonder

WHAT'S INSIDE?

Hi, I'm Zazzy Dot, your activity buddy.

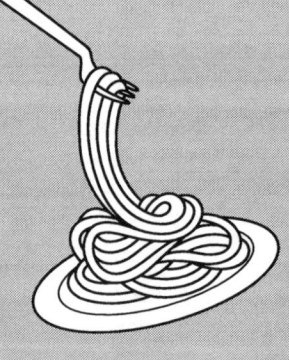

I like spaghetti, crunchy snacks, fun adventures, and things that fly.

I **LOVE** brain games.

Are you ready to have some fun?

Let's take a trip around

OUR BIG, BEAUTIFUL WORLD

Our planet has...

$3+3+1=$

☐

continents

What comes next?

10 · 9 · 8 · 7 · 6

[ ]

oceans

[ ][ ][ ]

countries

9

Pack your bags to
VISIT EVERY CONTINENT

HELLO, WORLD!

1. **North America**
2. **South America**
3. **Africa**
4. **Europe**
5. **Asia**
6. **Australia & Oceania**
7. **Antarctica**

1 _ _ _ _ _ _
_ _ _ _ _ _ _

ATLANTIC OCEAN

PACIFIC OCEAN

2 _ _ _ _ _ _
_ _ _ _ _ _

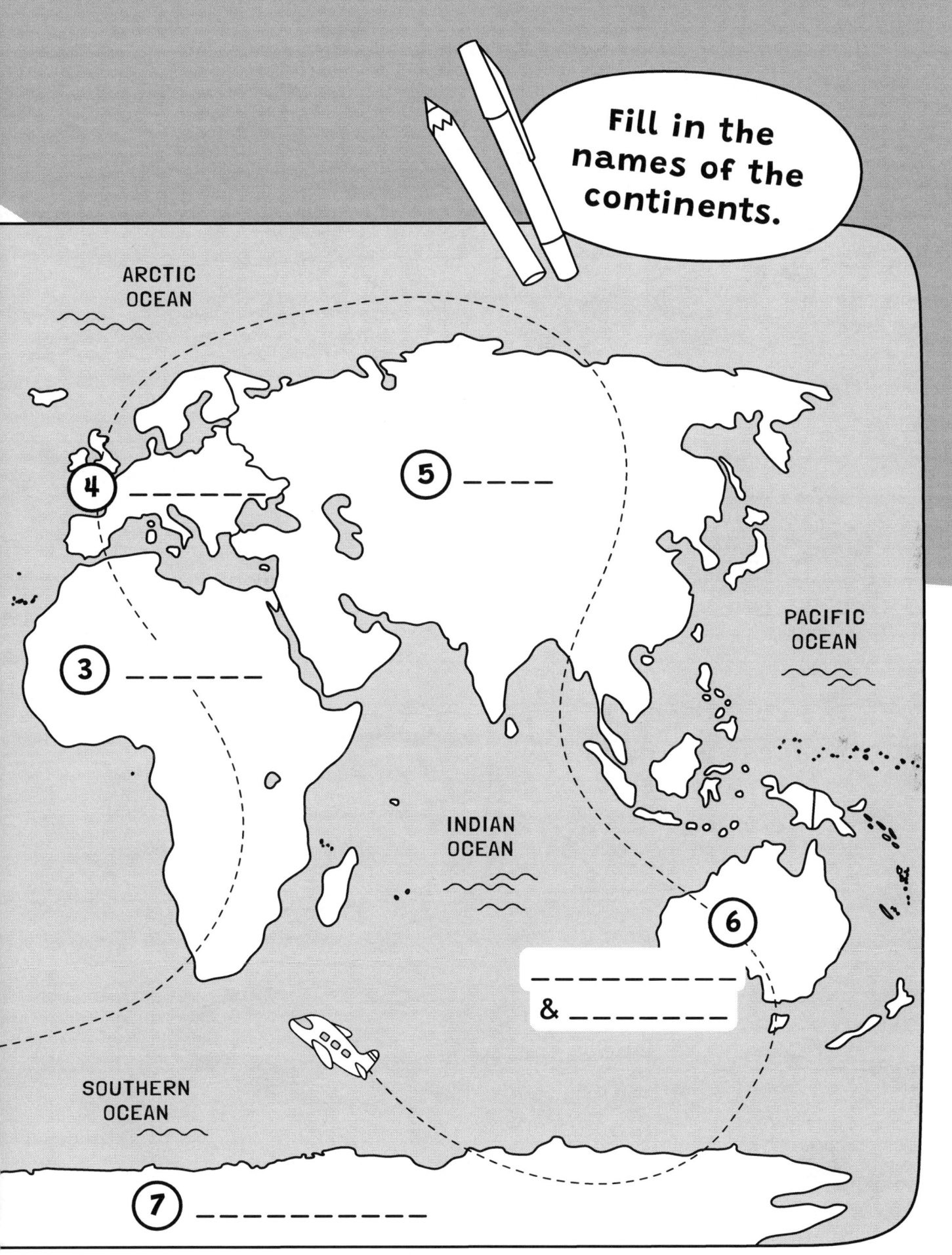

NORTH AMERICA

FACTS & FUNNIES

The country with the most pet dogs and cats is the USA.

Most maple syrup comes from Canada. It's made from the sap of the maple tree.

Knock, knock.
Who's there?
Alaska.
Alaska who?
Alaska to open the door again.

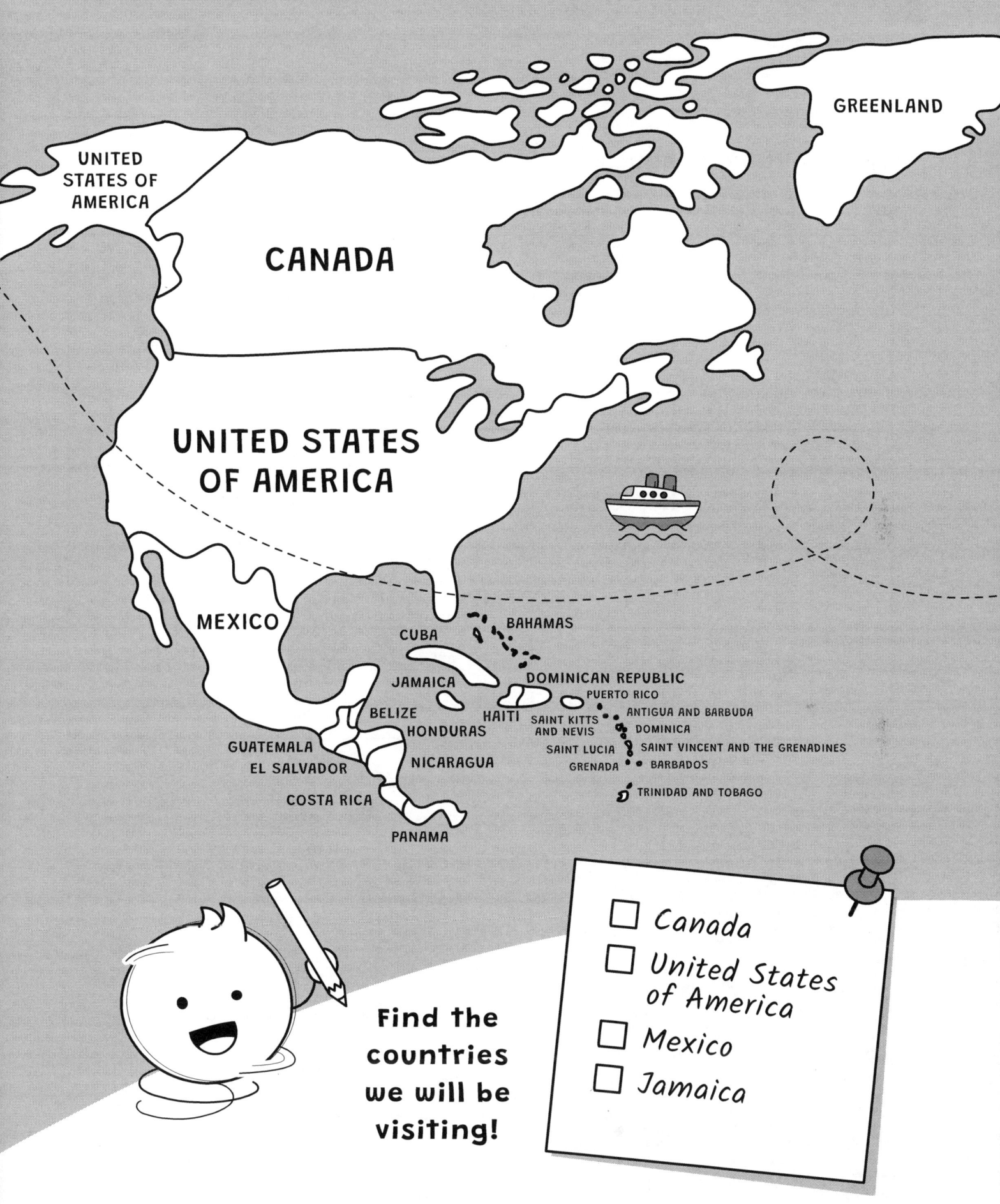

Find the countries we will be visiting!

- [ ] Canada
- [ ] United States of America
- [ ] Mexico
- [ ] Jamaica

Dino dig

Find all the dinosaurs.

```
P  A  R  P  K  J  S  T  E  G  O  S  A  U  R  U  S
T  Y  R  A  N  N  O  S  A  U  R  U  S  R  E  X  B
E  Q  K  I  B  Z  X  Y  H  D  F  J  K  Y  Z  O  F
R  J  C  N  B  V  E  L  O  C  I  R  A  P  T  O  R
A  P  A  T  O  S  A  U  R  U  S  N  I  X  C  B  J
N  W  L  Z  K  V  U  F  X  Z  Y  J  K  Z  H  O  B
O  Y  A  N  K  Y  L  O  S  A  U  R  U  S  I  N  E
D  K  O  K  B  R  A  C  H  I  O  S  A  U  R  U  S
O  J  G  Y  F  M  K  F  E  I  K  N  T  D  G  P  E
N  E  J  T  R  I  C  E  R  A  T  O  P  S  M  E  S
```

Did you know?
You can see many dinosaur bones in Canada's Dinosaur Provincial Park.

Stegosaurus

Tyrannosaurus rex

Ankylosaurus

Apatosaurus ✓

Triceratops

Brachiosaurus

Velociraptor

Pteranodon

Canada

SALUT!

CN Tower

Ice hockey

Maple Syrup

Beaver

1	Red	3	Skin	5	Brown	7	Light blue
2	Light green	4	Tan	6	Dark brown	8	Gray

Space explorers

Connect the dots.

Did you know? American astronauts were the first to land on the moon!

United States of America

1 Red	3 Light blue	5 Gold	7 Light brown
2 Dark blue	4 Skin	6 Brown	8 Black

Climbing high

Draw the right side of the famous pyramid in Mexico.

Did you know?
The pyramid at Chichen Itza has 365 steps — one for every day of the year!

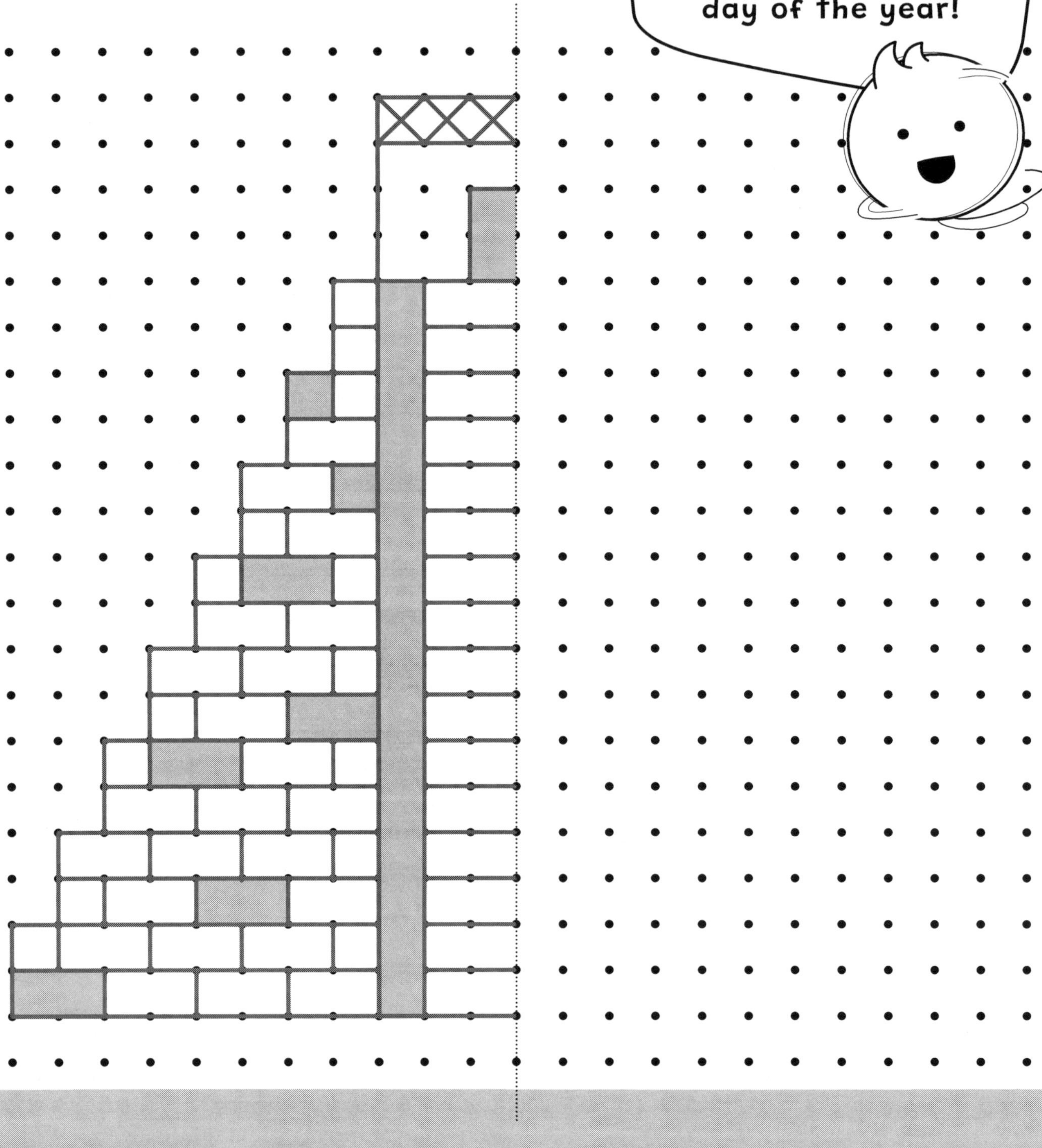

Mexico

1	Red	3	Light green	5	Gold	7	Light Brown
2	Dark green	4	Skin	6	Yellow	8	Black

19

Beach beats

Let's write a reggae song!

Party time

It's party time

Let's have some _____

Playing our music

In the _____

We're going to dance

Till the day is _____

Mama has cake

And gifts to be _____

Are you ready now?

Three, two, _____ !

Did you know?
Reggae music was invented in Jamaica.

done   won

one   fun   sun

Add this word to the CODE BREAKER on page 121.

Jamaica

Hummingbird

Reggae music

ELLO!

Usain Bolt
World's fastest sprinter!

| 1 | Green | 3 | Black | 5 | Red | 7 | Brown |
| 2 | Yellow | 4 | Orange | 6 | Skin | 8 | Light blue |

SOUTH AMERICA

HERE WE COME

FACTS & FUNNIES

Color me!

South America is the only continent where you can see pink dolphins.

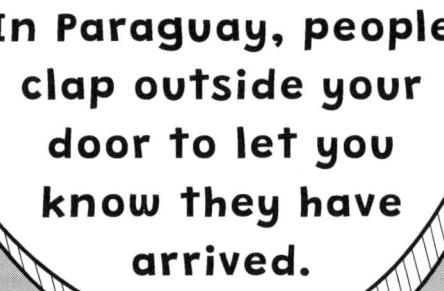

In Paraguay, people clap outside your door to let you know they have arrived.

What did the daddy volcano say to his son volcano?

I lava you!

VENEZUELA
GUYANA
SURINAME
FRENCH GUIANA
COLOMBIA
EQUADOR
BRAZIL
PERU
BOLIVIA
PARAGUAY
CHILE
ARGENTINA
URUGUAY
FALKLAND ISLANDS

Find the countries we will be visiting!

☐ Brazil
☐ Argentina
☐ Chile

Keeping score

Which is the best player on the Brazilian team?
Add up the numbers to find out.

Pedro

STRENGTH	9
SPEED	7
GOALS	3 +

Gabriel

STRENGTH	8
SPEED	5
GOALS	2 +

Clara

STRENGTH	6
SPEED	9
GOALS	1 +

SOCCER ? FOOTBALL

Did you know?
It's called **soccer** in the USA, Canada, and Australia, but in many countries, like Brazil, the game is called **football**.

24

Brazil

Toco toucan

Coffee

Christ the Redeemer

ORDEM E PROGRESSO

Rio Carnival

OLÁ!

Golden Trumpet

| 1 | Green | 3 | Dark blue | 5 | Skin | 7 | Orange |
| 2 | Yellow | 4 | Light blue | 6 | Black | 8 | Brown |

25

Smart Dot
Good for the planet, good for me

Forests clean the air we breathe.

To help preserve our forests, Zazzy is careful not to waste paper, which comes from trees.

Use again

Recycle

Amazing Amazon

Did you know?
The Amazon is the largest forest in the world. It's eight times the size of Texas!

VENEZUELA

GUYANA
SURINAME
FRENCH GUIANA

COLOMBIA

ECUADOR

Amazon forest

BRAZIL

PERU

BOLIVIA

Besides amazing plants and animals, hundreds of tribes also live in the Amazon.

Help Callie the caiman find
her way down the Amazon
river to her favorite rock.

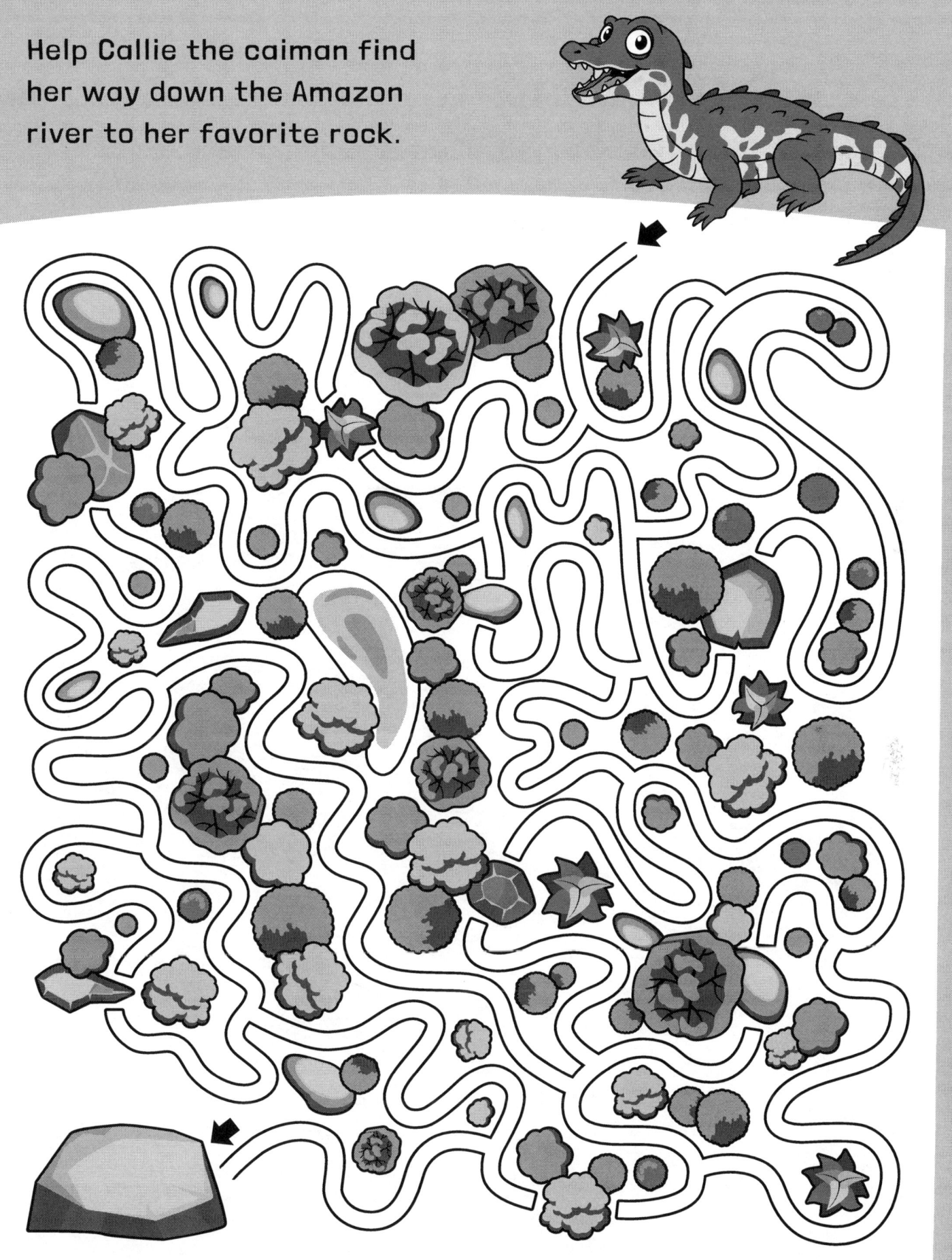

Let's go tango!

Complete the crossword puzzle of dancing styles.

Did you know?
Tango is a ballroom dance that was invented in Argentina.

rumba ✓	tango
samba	cha cha
mambo	bolero
salsa	merengue

28

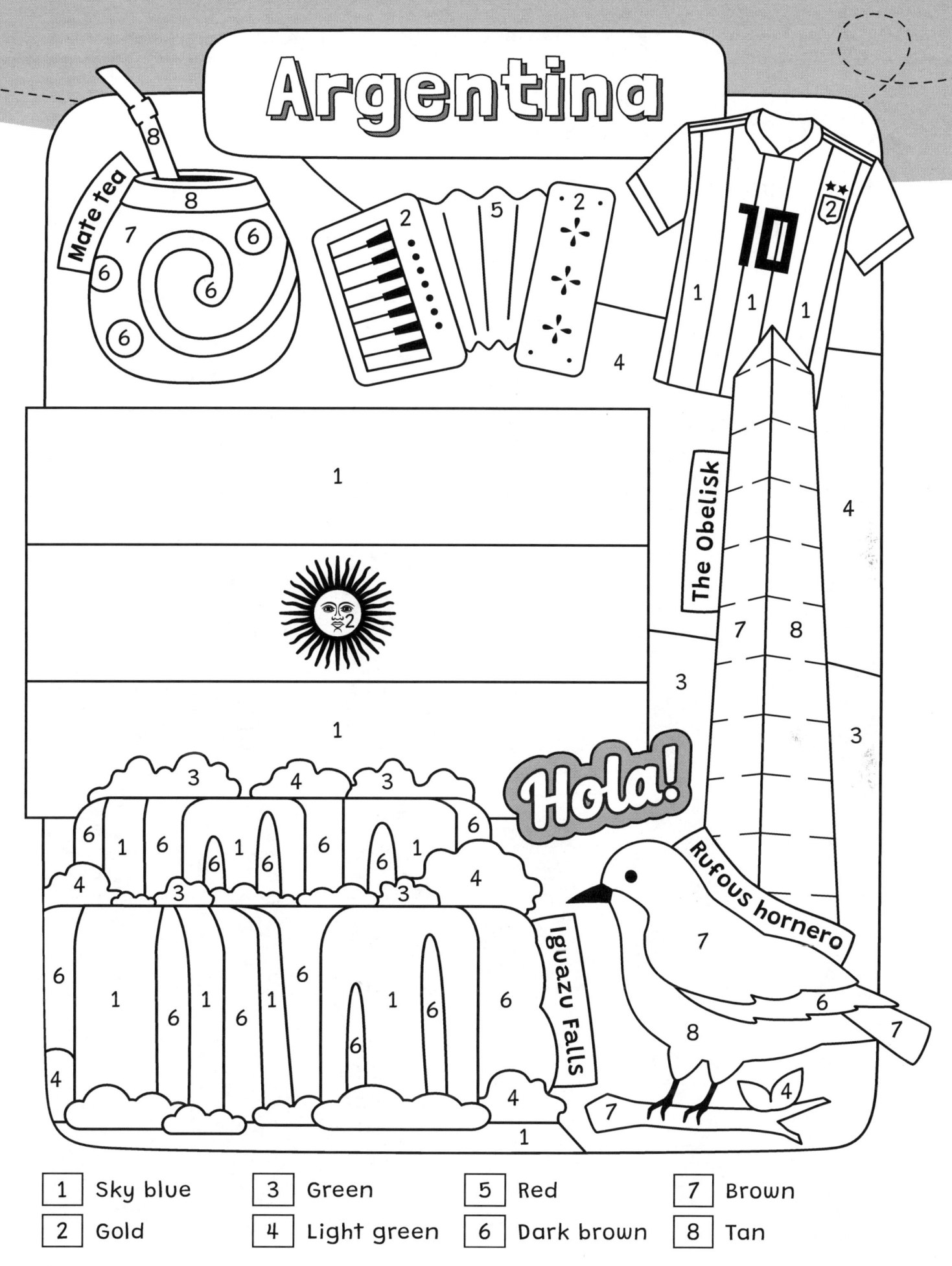

Argentina

Mate tea

The Obelisk

Hola!

Iguazu Falls

Rufous hornero

| 1 | Sky blue | 3 | Green | 5 | Red | 7 | Brown |
| 2 | Gold | 4 | Light green | 6 | Dark brown | 8 | Tan |

Face to face

Match each pair of identical statues.
Which statue is the odd one out?

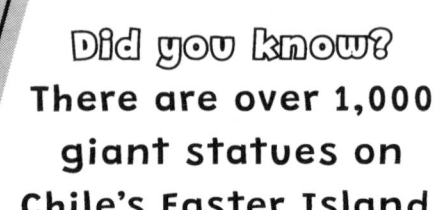

Did you know?
There are over 1,000
giant statues on
Chile's Easter Island.

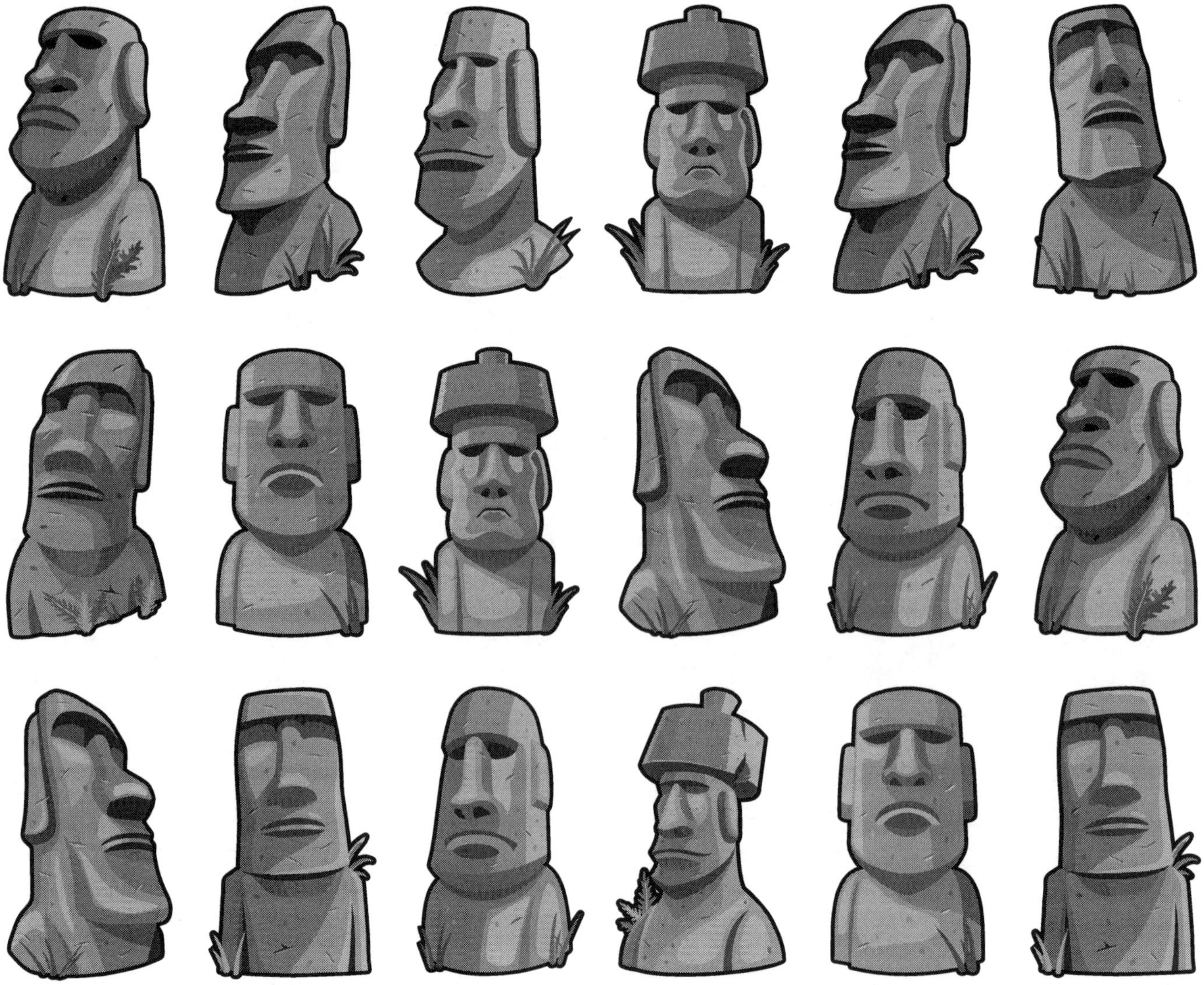

Chile

HOLA!

Andes mountains

South Andean deer

Hand of the Desert

| 1 | Dark blue | 3 | Red | 5 | Light brown | 7 | Gray |
| 2 | Sky blue | 4 | Skin | 6 | Tan | 8 | Black |

AFRICA

HERE WE COME

FACTS & FUNNIES

Victoria Falls in Africa is the largest waterfall in the world. It's twice as tall as Niagara Falls!

Giraffes hum to communicate with each other.

What time is it when a lion walks into a room?

Time to leave.

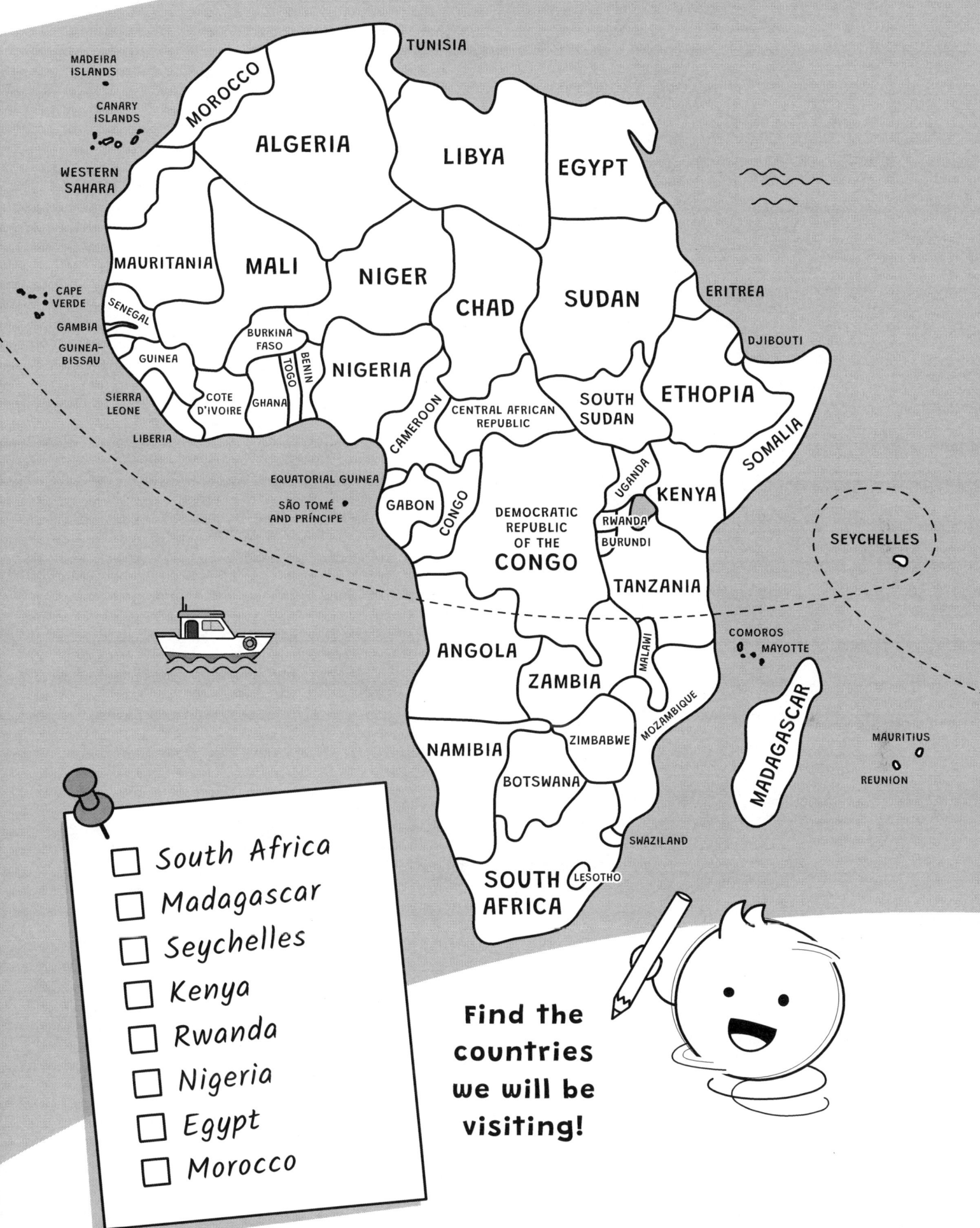

- ☐ South Africa
- ☐ Madagascar
- ☐ Seychelles
- ☐ Kenya
- ☐ Rwanda
- ☐ Nigeria
- ☐ Egypt
- ☐ Morocco

Find the countries we will be visiting!

Spotlight on numbers

Put the numbers in the correct order.

Did you know?
Because it's on the tip of the continent, South Africa has many lighthouses to guide ships at night.

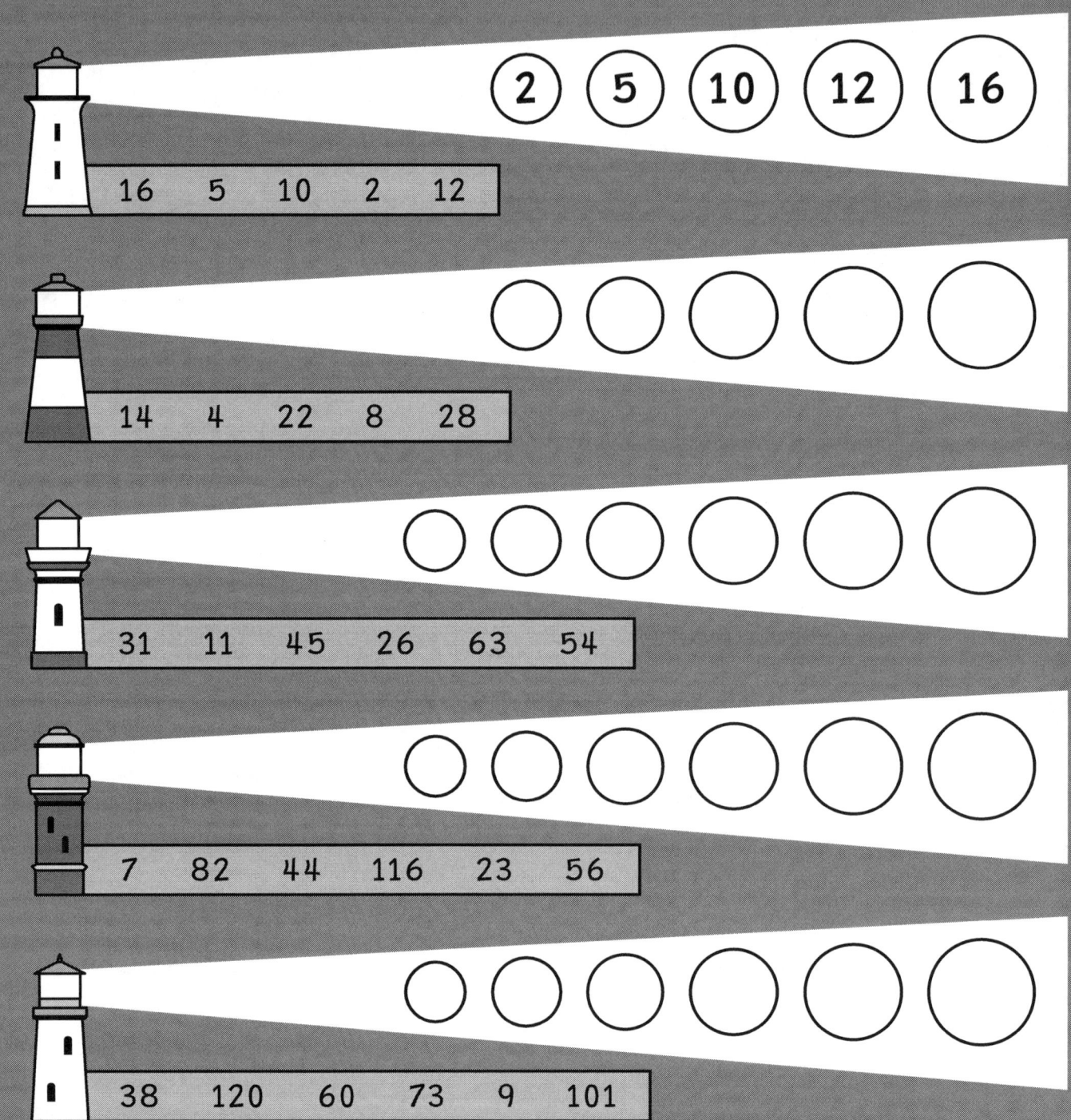

(2) (5) (10) (12) (16)

16   5   10   2   12

14   4   22   8   28

31   11   45   26   63   54

7   82   44   116   23   56

38   120   60   73   9   101

South Africa

1 Dark blue
2 Sky blue
3 Red
4 Forest green
5 Gold
6 Skin
7 Light brown
8 Black

Island adventure

Fill in the blanks to complete the story.

Last _____ , I traveled
with my _____ to Madagascar.
It was so beautiful.

On the first day, we swam in the
_____ and built a sandcastle.

On the second day, I saw a lemur!
He had a long _____ with black
and white _____ .

On the third _____ , we sailed in
a _____ around the island.

It was the best _____ ever.

day

tail

boat

ocean

family

stripes

summer

vacation

**Add this word to the
CODE BREAKER on page 121.**

Madagascar

Chameleon

Baobab tree

SALAMA!

Queen's Palace

Tomato frog

Lemur

| 1 | Red | 3 | Light green | 5 | Light brown | 7 | Gray |
| 2 | Green | 4 | Sky blue | 6 | Yellow | 8 | Black |

Time to pack

Circle the items you would pack for a beach holiday.

38

Seychelles

allo!

Black parrot

Giant tortoise

Hindu temple

| 1 | Green | 3 | Red | 5 | Dark blue | 7 | Light brown |
| 2 | Skin | 4 | Yellow | 6 | Sky blue | 8 | Black |

39

Spot me

Add the correct stripes or spots to the animals.

Did you know? The cheetah is the world's fastest land animal.

| Giraffe | Zebra | Cheetah | Tiger |

Kenya

Great Migration

jambo!

Lilac-breasted roller

East African lion

1	Green	3	Gold	5	Brown	7	Pink
2	Red	4	Skin	6	Sky blue	8	Black

The good traveler

Zazzy is always respectful when visiting new countries.

How can we be better travelers?

Reading about the destination

☐ YES ☐ NO

Learning new words

jambo! Privit! Ni Hao!

☐ YES ☐ NO

Littering

☐ YES ☐ NO

Respecting different cultures

☐ YES ☐ NO

Making fun of people

☐ YES ☐ NO

Where would you like to travel?

I would like to travel to _____

because:

1. _____

_____

2. _____

_____

3. _____

_____

Primate puzzler

Find the different types of primates.

```
C  H  I  M  P  A  N  Z  E  E
K  U  J  P  X  G  U  O  B  X
L  M  G  L  W  I  H  R  D  M
D  A  F  E  H  B  N  A  A  O
E  N  D  M  K  B  W  N  E  N
S  K  S  U  T  O  E  G  H  K
V  Z  P  R  W  N  D  U  F  E
G  O  R  I  L  L  A  T  C  Y
H  B  A  B  O  O  N  A  V  G
B  O  N  O  B  O  V  N  O  K
```

Did you know? Mountain gorillas live in protected areas in Rwanda and other African countries.

CHIMPANZEE

BABOON

GORILLA

ORANGUTAN

GIBBON

BONOBO

HUMAN

LEMUR

MONKEY

Rwanda

MURAHO!

Volcanoes National Park

King's Palace Museum

Leopard

| 1 | Sky blue | 3 | Dark green | 5 | Skin | 7 | Light brown |
| 2 | Yellow | 4 | Red | 6 | Brown | 8 | Black |

45

Fantastic fabric

Fill in the empty boxes to complete the Nigerian pattern.

Did you know?
Every country has its own traditional colors and patterns.

Nigeria

Kóyo!

African swallowtail

Udu jug

Black crowned crane

National Theater

| 1 | Green | 3 | Gold | 5 | Brown | 7 | Skin |
| 2 | Light green | 4 | Orange | 6 | Red | 8 | Black |

47

Mystery markings

Crack the code to discover the name
of the most famous Egyptian pharaoh.

Add this
word to the
CODE BREAKER
on page 121.

48

Egypt

Pyramids of Giza

Great Sphinx

Falafel

MARHABA!

Camel

Nile River

1	Red	3	Green	5	Sky blue	7	Light brown
2	Gold	4	Light green	6	Skin	8	Black

49

Morocco

Tagine pot

Spices

Salamu alaikum!

Jemaa el Fna market

| 1 | Red | 3 | Yellow | 5 | Skin | 7 | Brown |
| 2 | Dark green | 4 | Sky blue | 6 | Light brown | | |

EUROPE

FACTS & FUNNIES

The smallest country in the world is called Vatican City. It's one-eighth the size of Central Park in New York City!

People in Switzerland eat more chocolate than in any other country.

Knock, knock.
  Who's there?
Europe.
  Europe who?
Europe to no good!

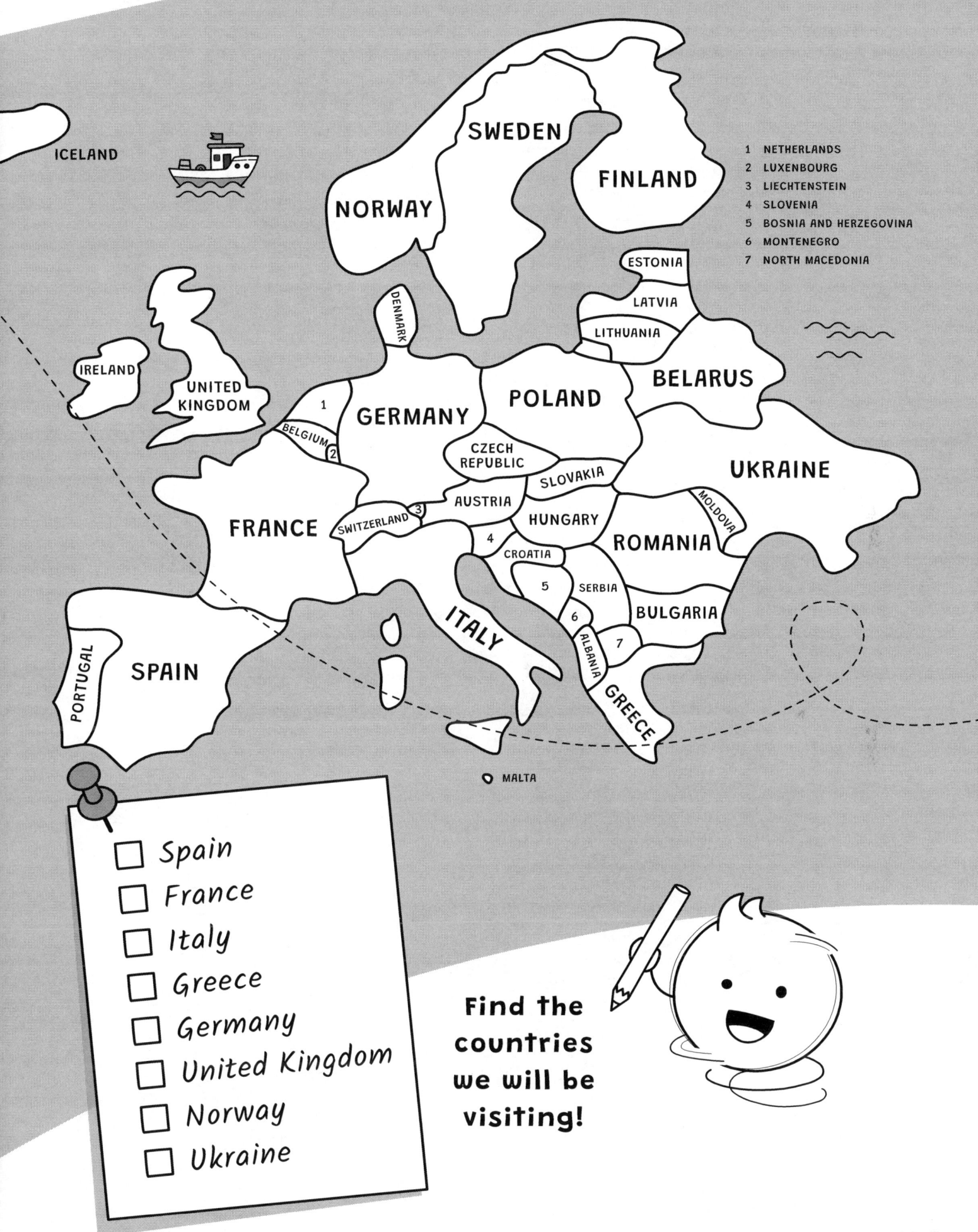

1 NETHERLANDS
2 LUXEMBOURG
3 LIECHTENSTEIN
4 SLOVENIA
5 BOSNIA AND HERZEGOVINA
6 MONTENEGRO
7 NORTH MACEDONIA

☐ Spain
☐ France
☐ Italy
☐ Greece
☐ Germany
☐ United Kingdom
☐ Norway
☐ Ukraine

Find the countries we will be visiting!

53

Mindful Me — Being present

Four people came to the Flamenco show.

Which one is being present?

Watching

Feeling

Listening

54

Spain

Churros

Castanets

Bull

hola!

Sagrada Familia

| 1 | Red | 3 | Sky blue | 5 | Light brown | 7 | Gray |
| 2 | Gold | 4 | Skin | 6 | Brown | 8 | Black |

Tower power

Connect the dots to reveal the French monument.

Did you know? It takes 50 painters a year and a half to repaint the Eiffel Tower.

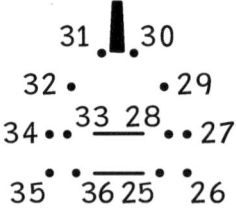

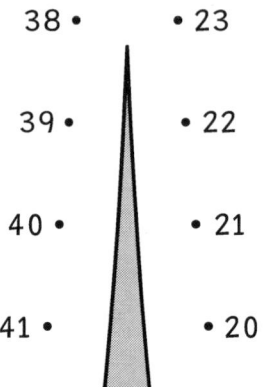
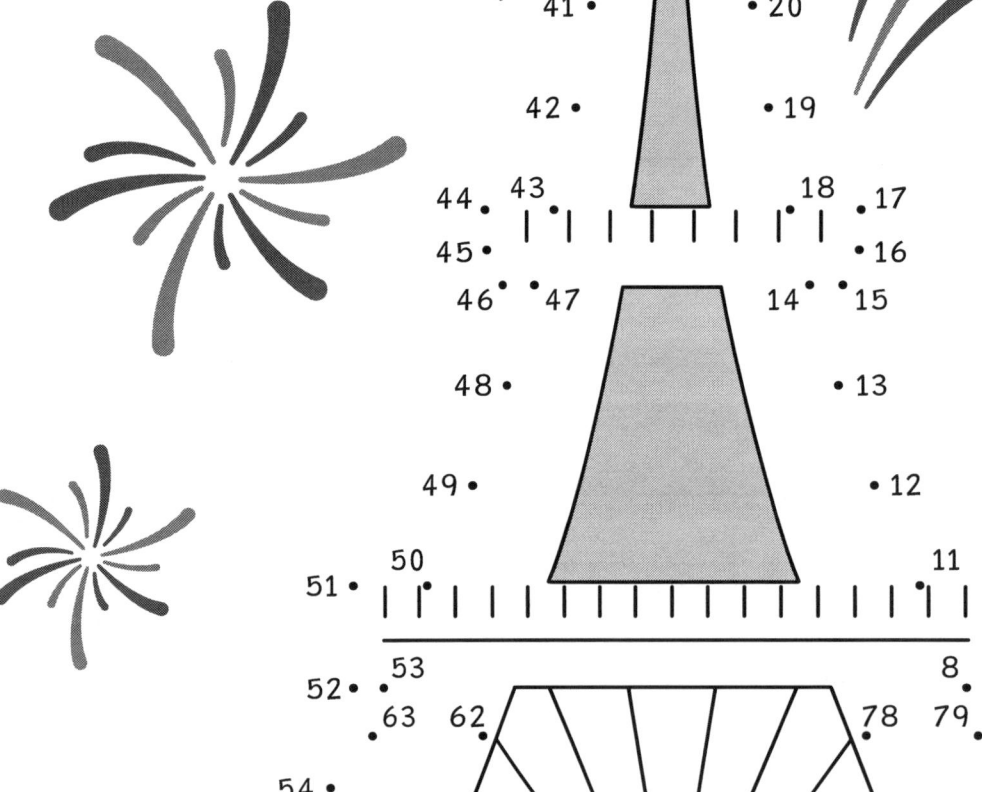

France

Croissant

Baguette

Salut!

Scientist Marie Curie

Arch of Triumph

Gallic rooster

| 1 | Red | 3 | Light blue | 5 | Light brown | 7 | Gray |
| 2 | Dark blue | 4 | Gold | 6 | Skin | 8 | Light green |

57

Seeing double

Find **11** differences between the real Mona Lisa and the fake.

Did you know? The Italian painter and inventor Leonardo da Vinci wrote backwards to keep his notes secret.

Italy

1	Red	3	Light blue	5	Light brown	7	Gray
2	Green	4	Gold	6	Skin	8	Purple

59

Go team!

Who will win the top medals at the Olympics? Add up the scores to find out.

2nd **1st** **3rd**

Did you know? The Olympic games started in Greece over 2,000 years ago.

41

38

Team China

+
___

45

37

Team Greece

+
___

36

44

Team USA

+
___

Greece

Acropolis

Geia!

Dolphin

Mykonos windmills

62

| 1 | Dark blue | 3 | Gold | 5 | Light brown |
| 2 | Sky blue | 4 | Dark brown | 6 | Cream |

Maestro of melody

Fill in the opposite of each word to reveal the answer to Zazzy's question.

DOWN → ▢ ▢

OUT → ▢ ▢

HAPPY → ▢ ▢ ▢

OVER → ▢ ▢ ▢ ▢ ▢

BOTTOM → ▢ ▢ ▢

Ludwig van Beethoven is a famous German musician. Which instrument did he play?

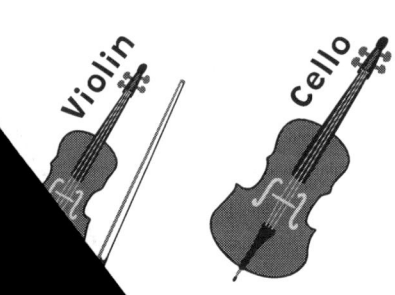 Violin

Cello

 Piano

 Guitar

Germany

Frankfurter sausages

Pretzel

Guten Tag!

Brandenburg Gate

| 1 | Yellow | 3 | Black | 5 | Light blue | 7 | Light brown |
| 2 | Red | 4 | Gray | 6 | Skin | 8 | Green |

Writer's delight

Fill in the rhyming words to complete the poem.

My book

book   way
me
find   there

Come and have a look
_____
I'm writing a _____
_____

I have so much to say
_____
In a very special _____
_____

I see words everywhere
_____
Stories here, stories _____
_____

I see them in my mind
_____
Imagine things I will _____
_____

I write what I see
_____
About you and about _____
_____

Did you know?
The famous English writer Jane Austen never signed her name on her books.

United Kingdom

Fish and chips

Big Ben

HELLO!

Bulldog

1	Red	3	Light blue	5	Light brown	7	Gray
2	Dark blue	4	Gold	6	Tan	8	Pink

Sea escape

Help Marty the mouse get to the top of the Viking ship.

Did you know? Thursday is named after the Viking god, Thor!

Eggs-pert designs

Draw the right side of the Pysanky eggs to complete the decorations.

Color the eggs when you're done.

Ukraine

Nightingale

Varenyky dumplings

Sunflower

Bandura

Privit!

| 1 | Dark blue | 3 | Yellow | 5 | Red | 7 | Light brown |
| 2 | Sky blue | 4 | Orange | 6 | Light green | 8 | Skin |

ASIA

HERE WE COME

RUSSIA

The Great Wall of China is so long, it would take one and a half years to walk across it.

KAZAKHSTAN

GEORGIA

UZBEKISTAN

TURKMENISTAN

TURKEY

CYPRUS

SYRIA

LEBANON

PALESTINE

IRAQ

IRAN

AFGHANISTAN

ISRAEL

JORDAN

BAHRAIN

QATAR

SAUDI ARABIA

OMAN

YEMEN

- ☐ Russia
- ☐ Turkey
- ☐ Jordan
- ☐ United Arab Emirates
- ☐ India
- ☐ China
- ☐ Japan
- ☐ Indonesia

Find the countries we will be visiting!

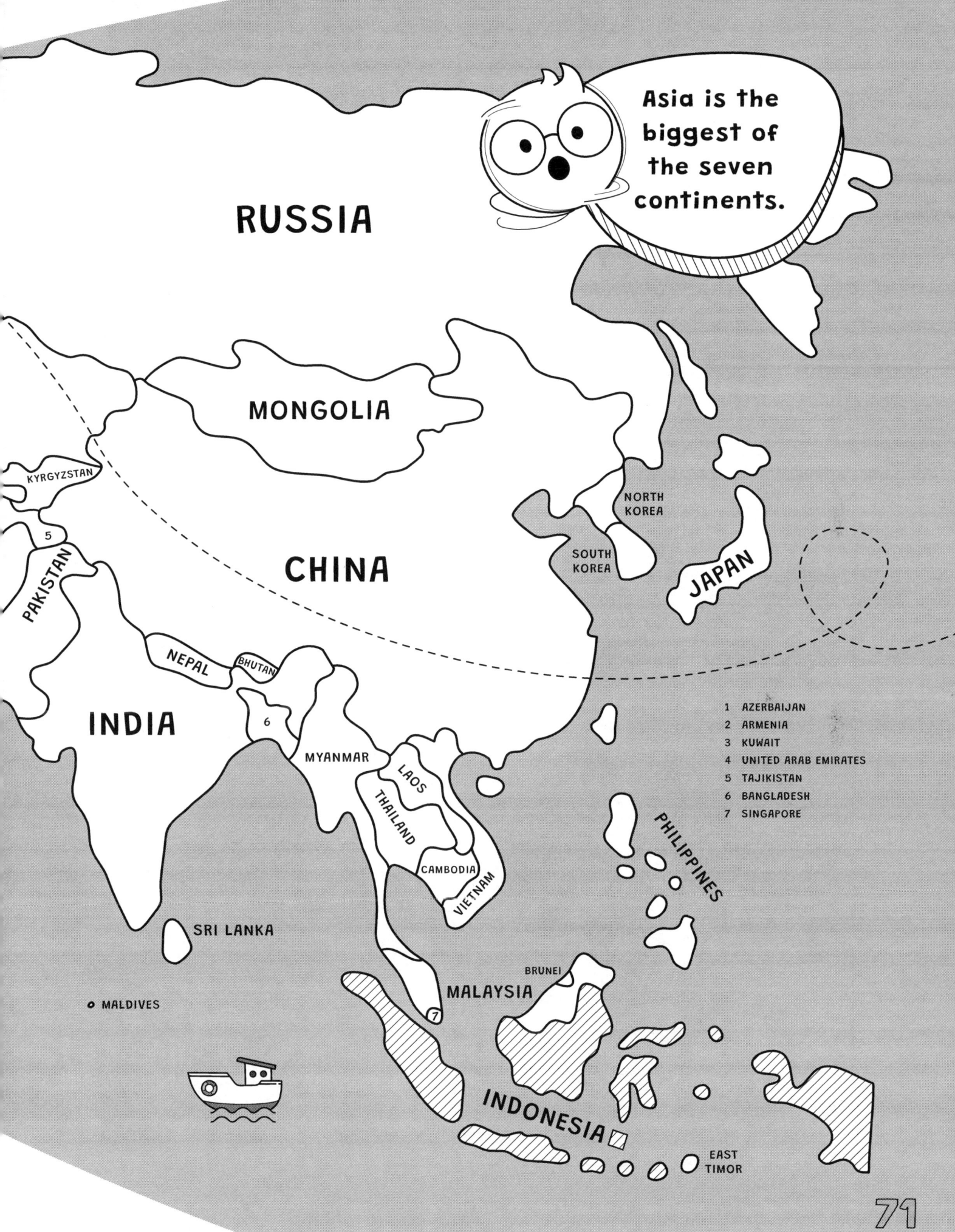

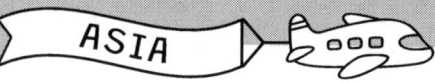

Map maker

Use the directions to travel across the map and write down what you find.

Did you know?
Russia is the biggest country in the world.

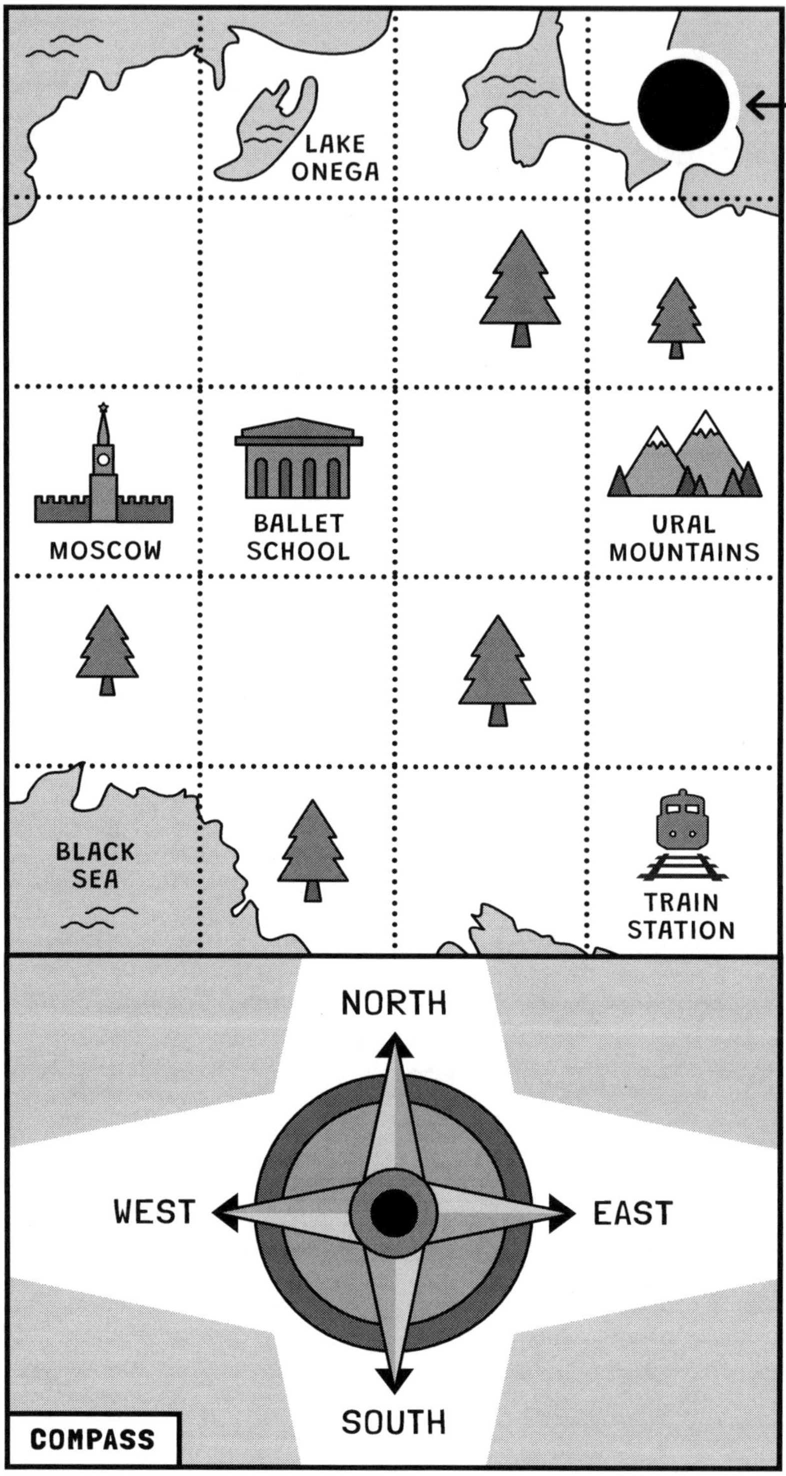

Start here.

LAKE ONEGA

MOSCOW

BALLET SCHOOL

URAL MOUNTAINS

BLACK SEA

TRAIN STATION

NORTH

WEST

EAST

SOUTH

COMPASS

Then go west twice.

Then go south twice.

Then go east twice.

Then go south twice.

Then go west three times.

Then go north twice.

72

Russia

Prevet!

Nesting dolls

Balalaika

Bear

Saint Basil's Cathedral

| 1 | Dark blue | 3 | Red | 5 | Brown | 7 | Skin |
| 2 | Sky blue | 4 | Gold | 6 | Light brown | 8 | Green |

73

Floating on air

Connect the dots to reveal a fun activity in Turkey.

15
14
39 40 56 57 81
13 16 38 58 80 82
41 55 83
12 17 37 59 79 84
18 42 54 78
36 60 85
11 44 52 77
19
10 35 43 53 51 61 86
20 45 76
9 34 46 50 62 87
21 75
8 33 47 49 63 74 88
22
32 48 64 73 89
7 23
31 65 90
6 24 72
5 25 30 66 71 91
4 26 29 67 70 92
3 27 28 68 69 93
1 95 94
2 97
100 101 96

99 98

Turkey

MERHABA!

Hagia Sophia

Whirling dervish

Gray wolf

Turkish delight

Fez

| 1 | Red | 3 | Tan | 5 | Orange | 7 | Gray |
| 2 | Sky blue | 4 | Pink | 6 | Skin | 8 | Black |

75

Ancient treasure

Millions of people visit the Treasury in Petra, Jordan.
Spot the 10 differences between the left and right side.

Jordan

marhaba!

Wadi Rum desert

Arabian oryx

Olives

Tablah

1	Red	3	Black	5	Sky blue	7	Orange
2	Green	4	Gray	6	Yellow	8	Skin

77

Record breaker

How tall is the Burj Khalifa? Add up the numbers to learn the answer.

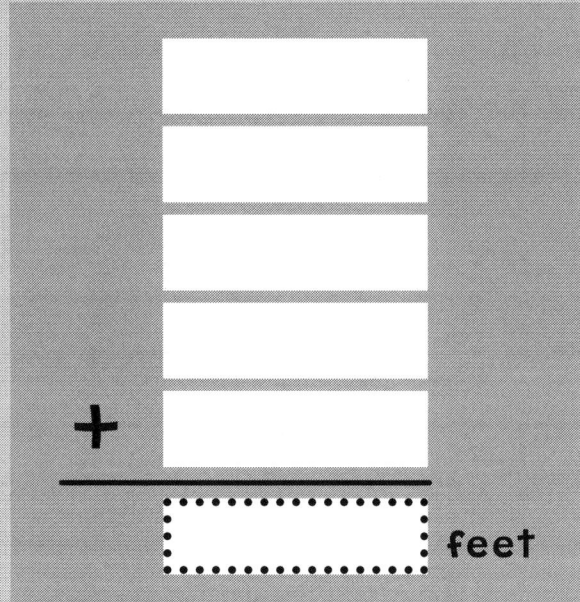

+

_____

feet

Did you know?
Burj Khalifa is the tallest building in the world. It has more than 160 floors!

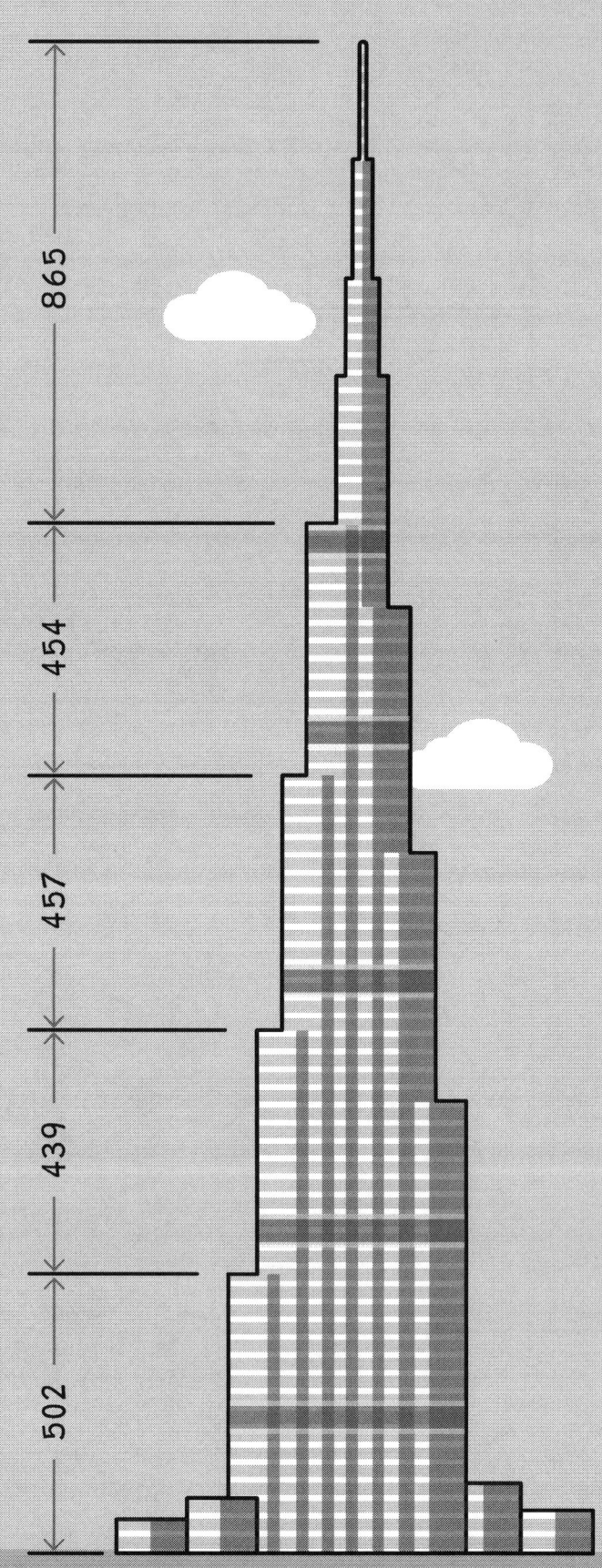

865

454

457

439

502

United Arab Emirates

Lantern

Falcon

Dates

Marhaba!

Sadu tent

1	Red	3	Black	5	Gold	7	Brown
2	Dark green	4	Gray	6	Orange	8	Skin

Chess challenge

Use the chessboard grid to fill in the blanks.

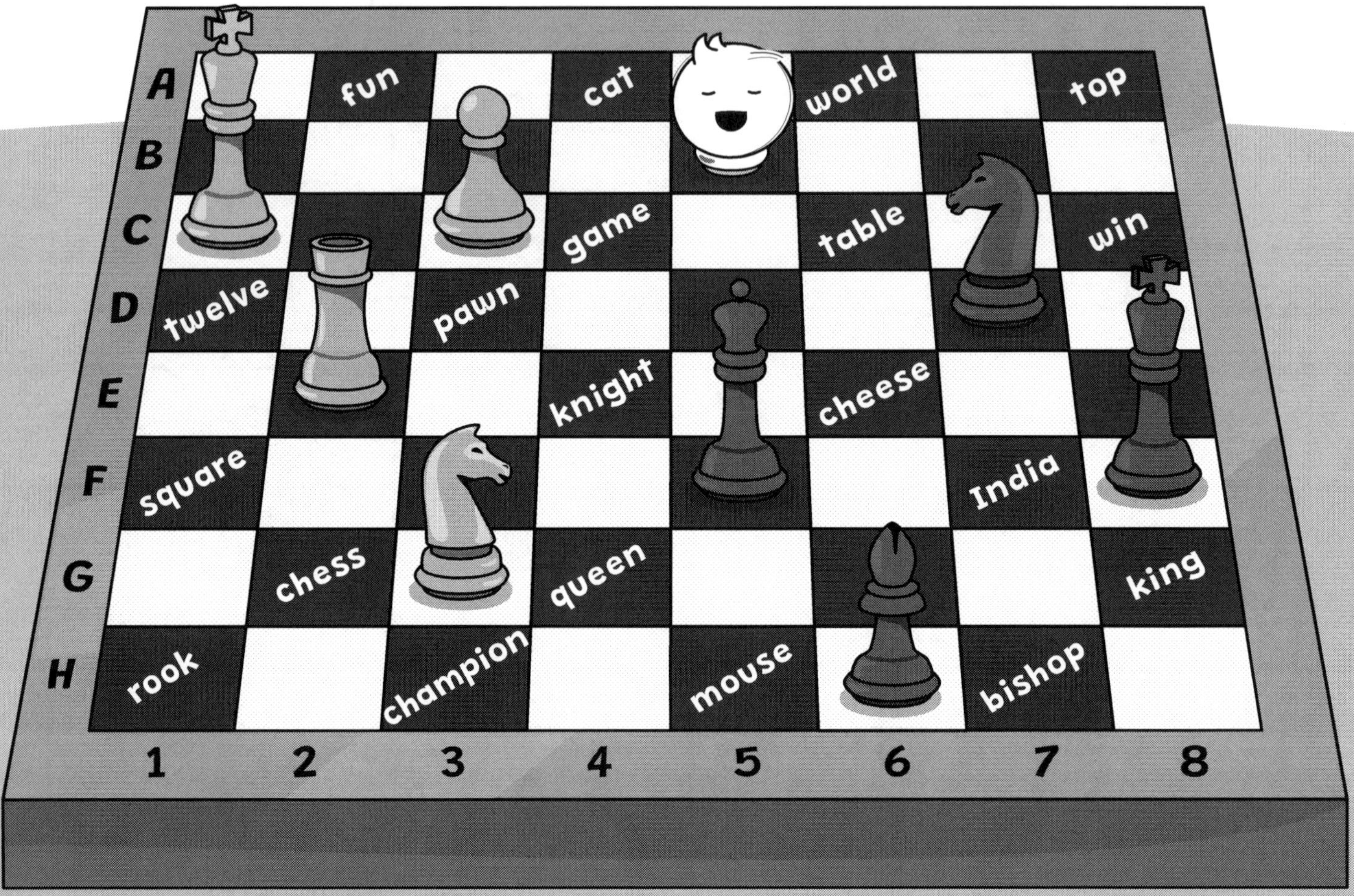

The _____ of _____ was invented in _____ .
　　　 C4　　　　　　 G2　　　　　　　　　　　　 F7

A chess _____ is called a grandmaster.
　　　　　 H3

The youngest grandmaster in the _____
　　　　　　　　　　　　　　　　　　　 A6
is _____ years old!
　　 D1

India

Taj Mahal

Holi festival

Samosas

NAMASTE!

Elephant

1	Orange	3	Gray	5	Skin	7	Yellow
2	Green	4	Blue	6	Pink	8	Light brown

Smart Dot
Good for the planet, good for me

Zazzy loves to learn about wild animals and all the ways we can help protect them.

Protecting the wild

Draw a wild animal in its habitat – the place where it lives.

Plants

Food

Water

Match the endangered animals to their names.

Lemur

Gorilla

Elephant

Rhinoceros

Tiger

Sea turtle

Koala

Whale

Orangutan

Panda portrait

Draw the missing half of the cute panda.

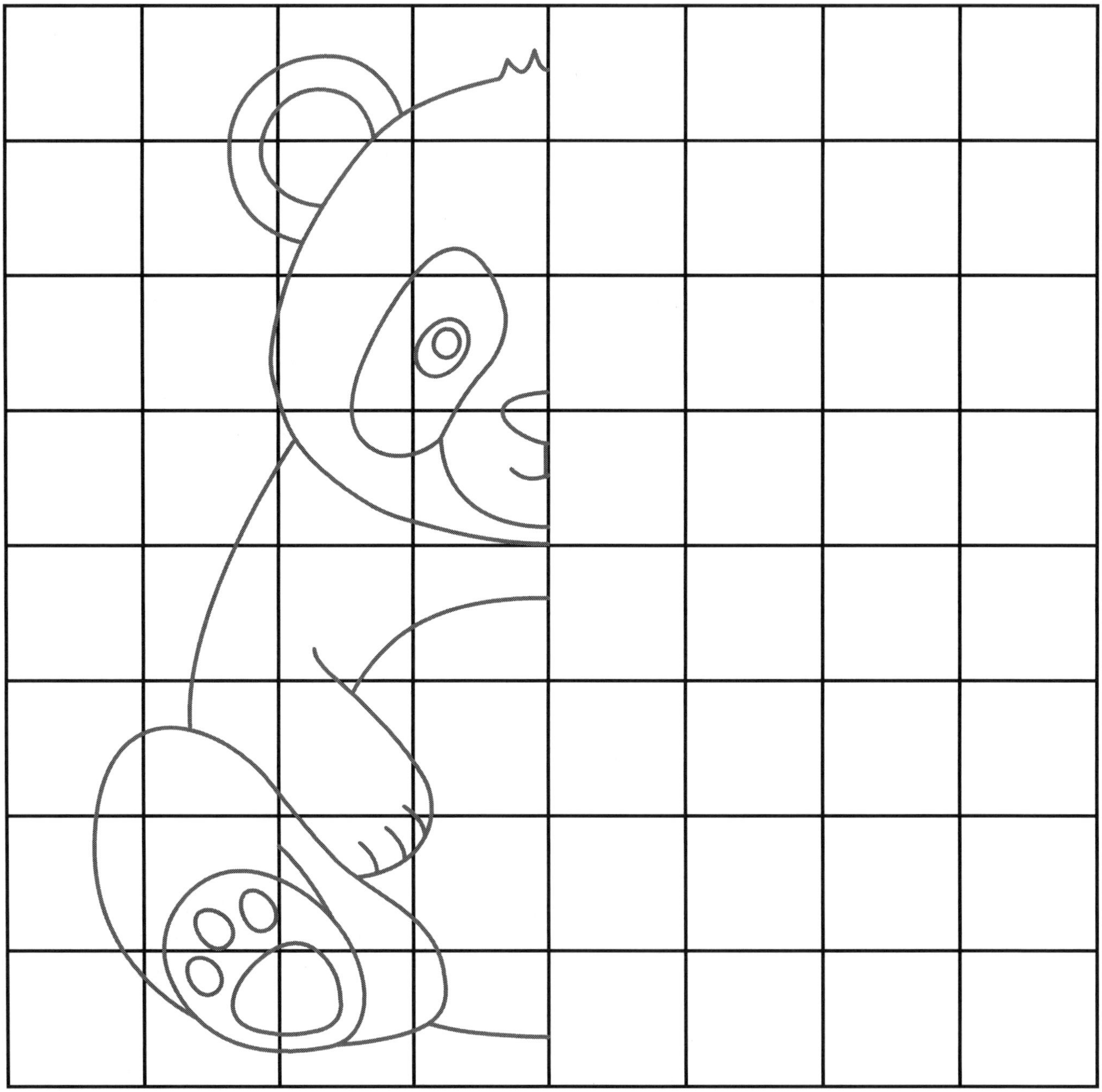

Did you know? Giant pandas are born pink and can fit in your hand.

China

Lantern

Great Wall of China

Ni Hao!

Kung fu

Noodles

New Year Festival

| 1 | Red | 3 | Gold | 5 | Light green | 7 | Light brown |
| 2 | Yellow | 4 | Green | 6 | Skin | 8 | Black |

85

Paper pup

Follow the instructions to make an origami dog.

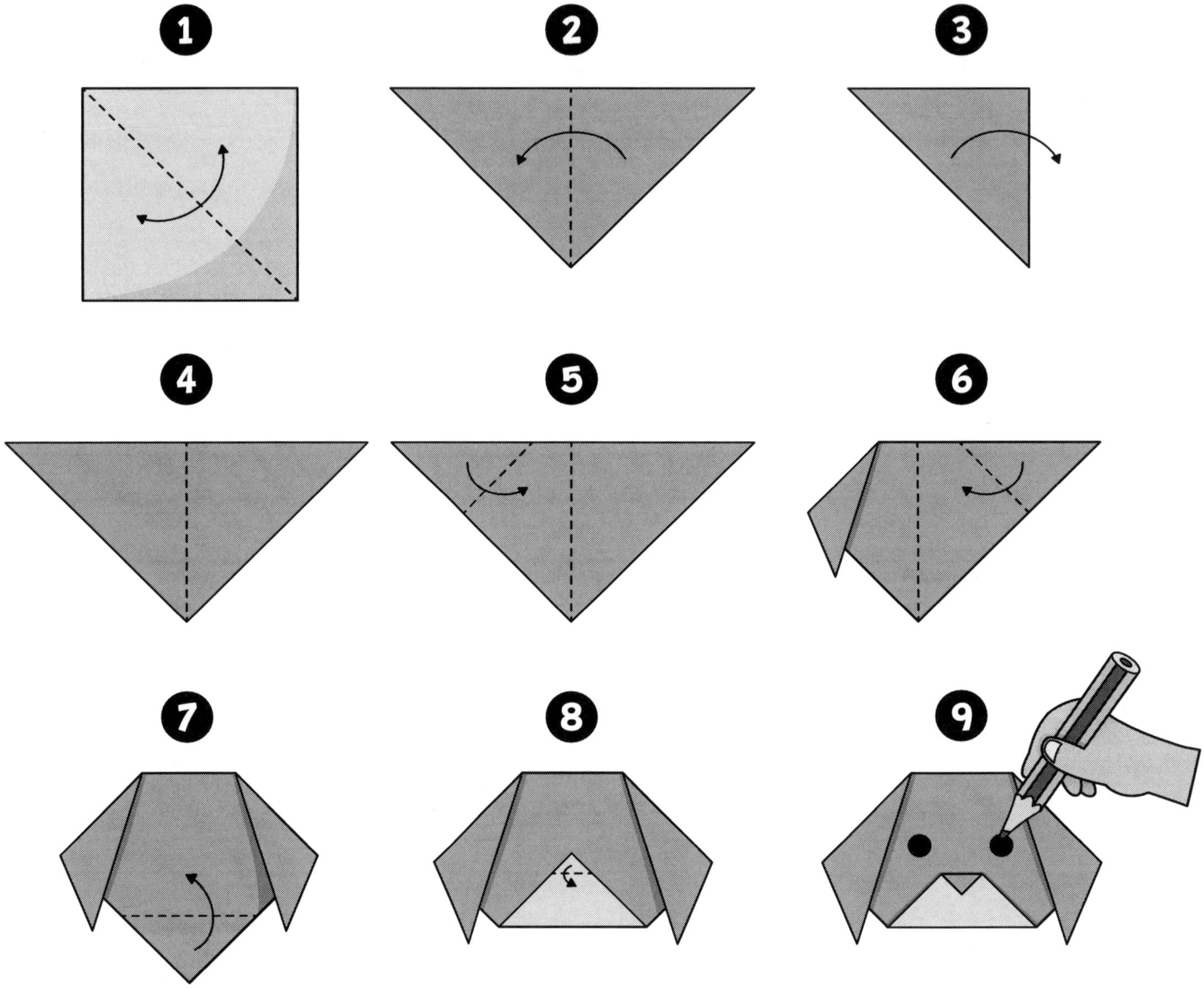

1

2

3

4

5

6

7

8

9

> **Did you know?**
> Hundreds of years ago, when paper was expensive, people gave each other origami art as gifts.

86

Japan

Origami

Sushi

Lucky cat

KONNICHIWA!

Kimono

Itsukushima Shrine

Mount Fuji

| 1 | Red | 3 | Gold | 5 | Light green | 7 | Gray |
| 2 | Yellow | 4 | Pink | 6 | Skin | 8 | Black |

87

Monkeying around

How many words can you make out of the monkeys' letters?

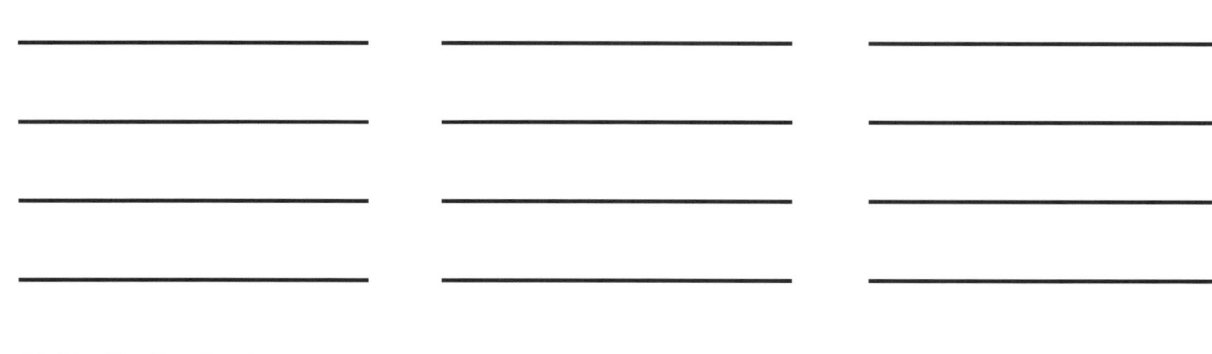

Pssst...
Try starting with
three-letter words first.

Indonesia

Becak taxi

Komodo dragon

HALO!

Borobudur temple

| 1 | Red | 3 | Gold | 5 | Brown | 7 | Gray |
| 2 | Light blue | 4 | Green | 6 | Skin | 8 | Light gray |

AUSTRALIA & OCEANIA

HERE WE COME

FACTS & FUNNIES

CIAO!

BONJOUR!

AHOJ!

HALO!

OLÁ!

Papua New Guinea has the most languages – 840 of them!

The biggest butterfly in the world is 12 inches across. That's bigger than a dinner plate!

How can you tell the ocean is friendly?

It waves.

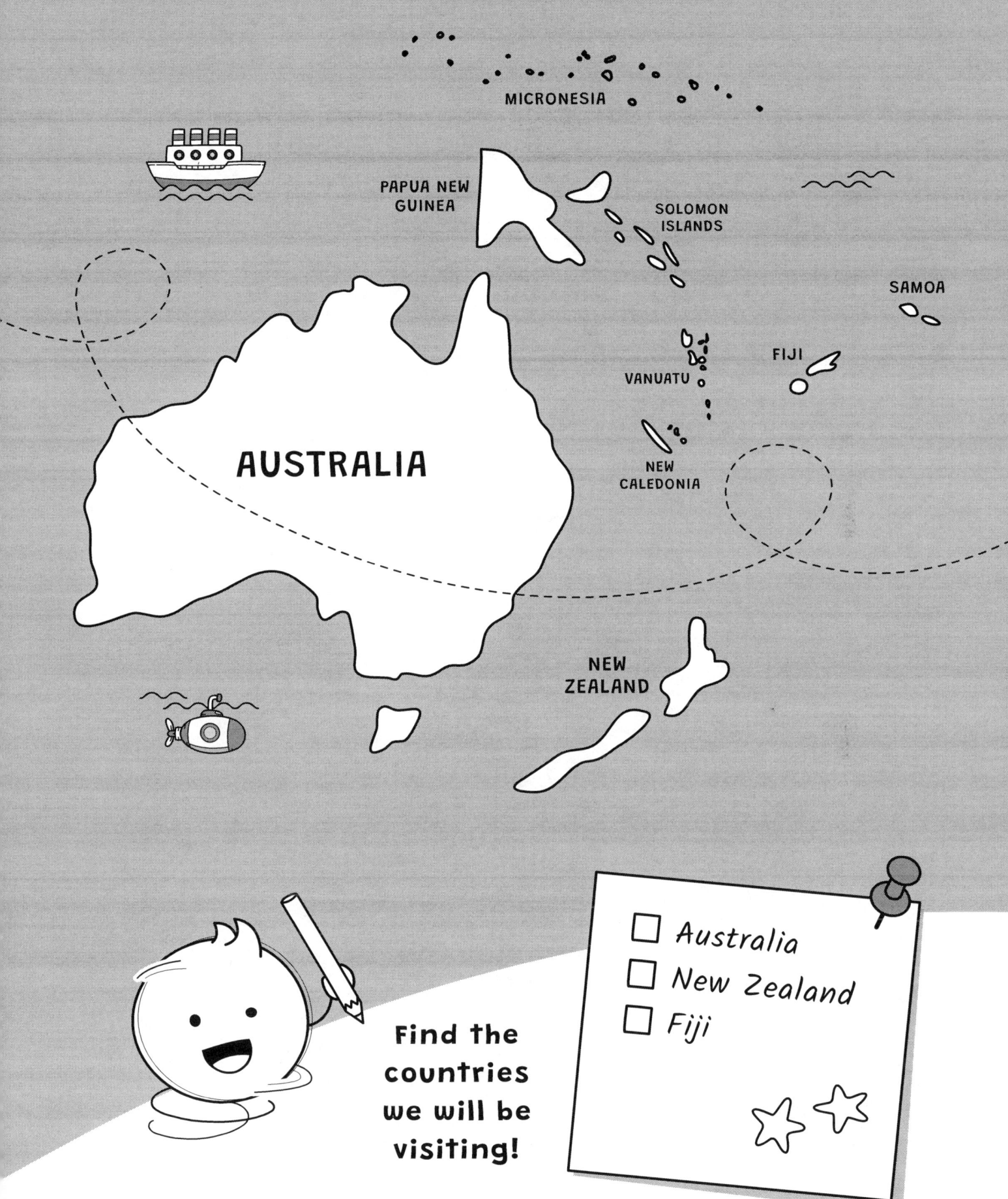

Find the countries we will be visiting!

- [ ] Australia
- [ ] New Zealand
- [ ] Fiji

Boomerang buddies

What number comes next?

Did you know?
If you throw a boomerang correctly, it will fly back to you.

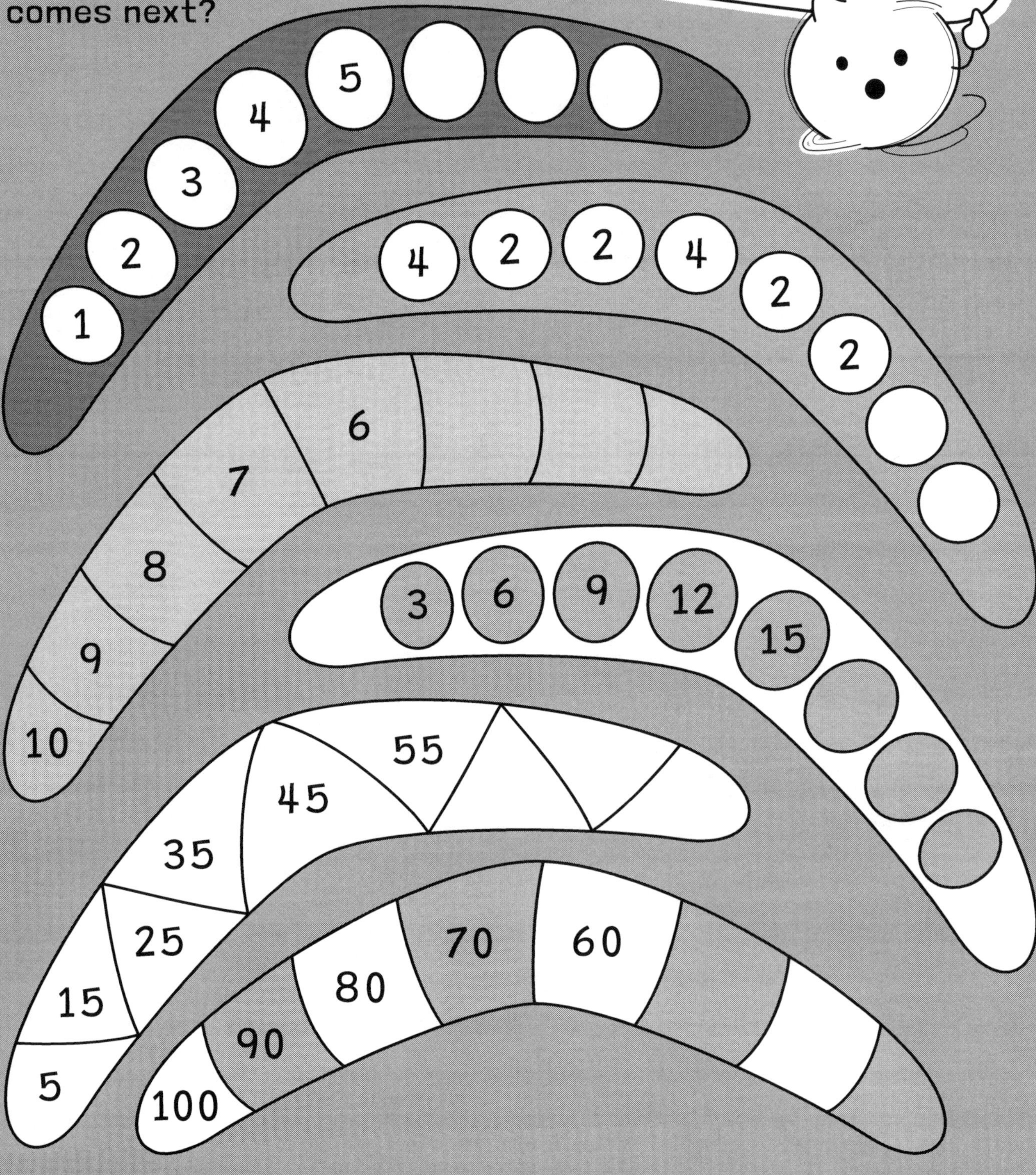

1 2 3 4 5 ◯ ◯ ◯

4 2 2 4 2 2 ◯ ◯

6 7 8 9 10

3 6 9 12 15 ◯ ◯ ◯ ◯

55 45 35 25 15 5

70 60

80

90

100

Australia

HELLO!

Sydney Opera House

Boomerang

Kangaroo

Pavlova

| 1 | Red | 3 | Light blue | 5 | Brown | 7 | Skin |
| 2 | Dark blue | 4 | Yellow | 6 | Light brown | 8 | Black |

93

Smart Dot
Good for the planet, good for me

Zazzy is careful not to harm the coral reef or any creature that lives there.

Cool coral reef

In the picture on the next page, count the creatures that live in the coral reef.

| | Corals | **2** | Sea urchins | | Starfish |

| | Fish | | Oysters | | Seahorses |

| | Stingrays | | Jellyfish | | Octopuses |

95

Village visit

Kai and Kuri are on their way to the beach to go fishing. Help them find their way through the Maori village.

New Zealand

Kiwi bird

Sky Tower

Kia Ora!

Kiwi

Rugby

1	Red	3	Light blue	5	Brown	7	Skin
2	Dark blue	4	Gold	6	Green	8	Black

Hitting the waves

Design your own surfboard.

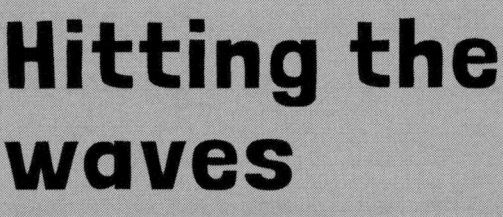

Did you know? Fiji is made up of over 330 islands!

| 1 | Red | 3 | Light blue | 5 | Green | 7 | Light brown |
| 2 | Dark blue | 4 | Yellow | 6 | Brown | 8 | Skin |

99

HERE WE COME

ANTARCTICA

FACTS & FUNNIES

Penguins are birds, but they can't fly. They use their wings to swim.

South Pole

Antarctica is the largest desert in the world – it's an ice desert!

Who is the penguin's favorite aunt?

Aunt Arctica

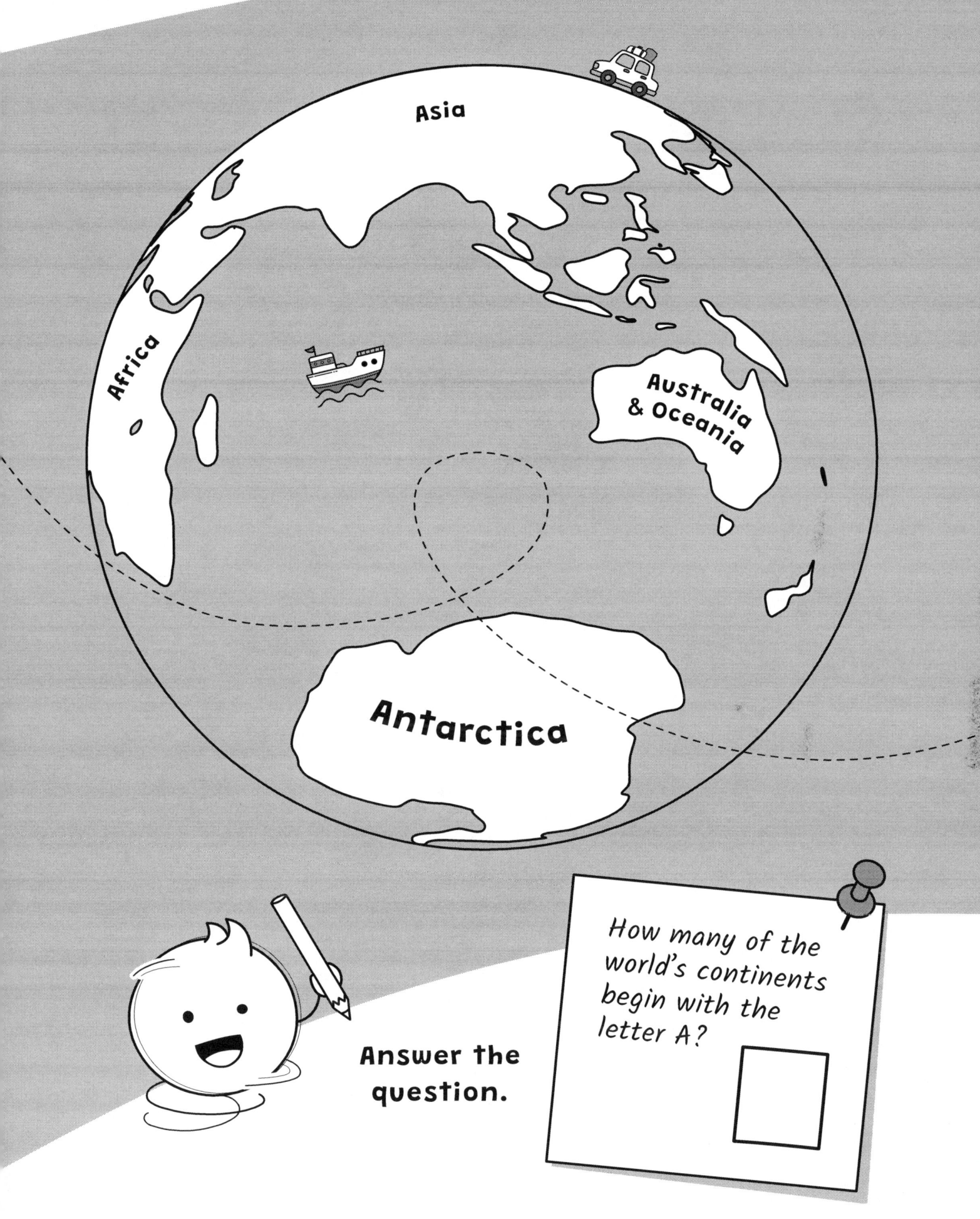

Asia

Africa

Australia & Oceania

Antarctica

Answer the question.

How many of the world's continents begin with the letter A?

Look who's chilling

Scientists have arrived by submarine to study Antarctica. Check off all the animals they see.

Petrel

Dolphin

Sea lion

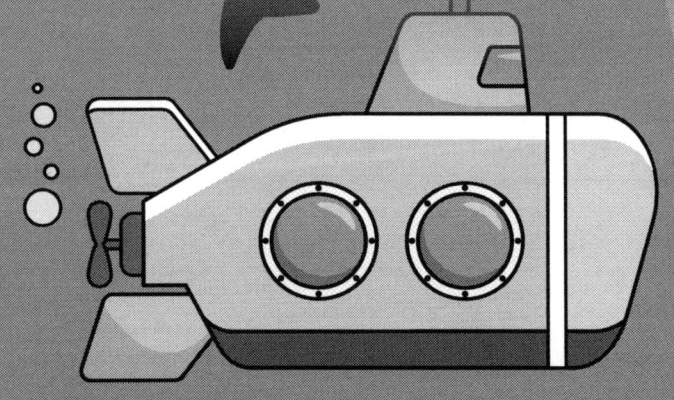

Icefish

☑ Petrel	☐ Icefish
☐ Tern	☐ Krill
☐ Albatross	☐ Starfish
☐ Whale	☐ Penguin
☐ Orca	☐ Gull
☐ Dolphin	☐ Seal
☐ Squid	☐ Sea lion

103

Photo album

Fill in the names of the countries in the photographs.

Kenya

Add this word to the
CODE BREAKER on page 121.

Souvenir sorter

Match the country stickers to the correct continents.

North America

South America

Africa

Europe

Asia

Australia & Oceania

Antarctica

Magnet mix-up

Unscramble the magnet letters to reveal six countries.

ADCANA _ _ _ _ _ _

INEGAIR _ _ _ _ _ _ _

TAIYL _ _ _ _ _

URTYEK _ _ _ _ _ _

HICAN _ _ _ _ _

IFIJ _ _ _ _

Make your own map!

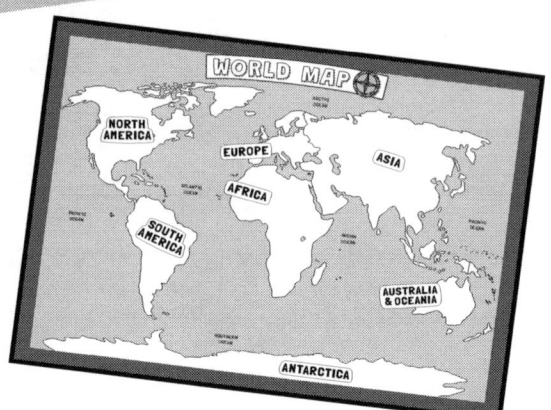

STEP 1 Cut out the four parts of the map, then tape the pages together.

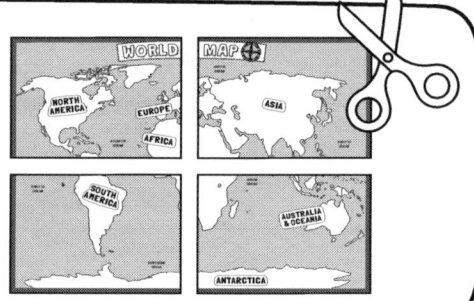

STEP 2 Color the map using this color key.

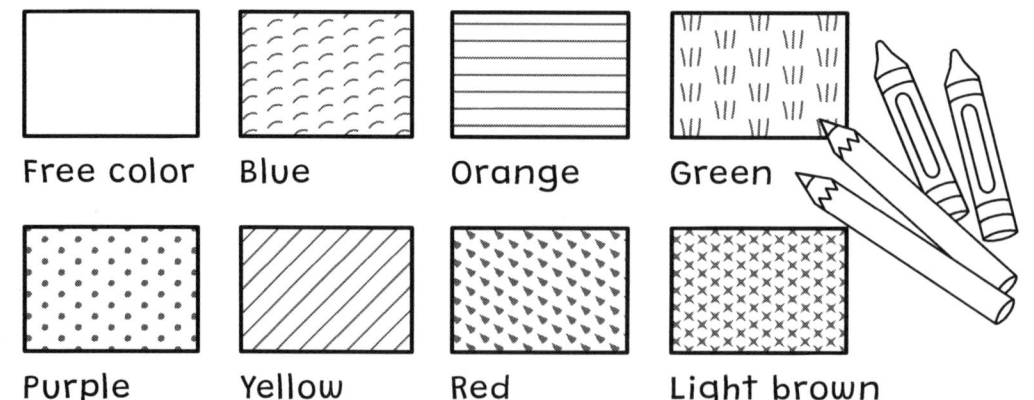

Free color   Blue   Orange   Green

Purple   Yellow   Red   Light brown

STEP 3 Color and cut out the items on pages **117** and **119**, then glue them onto the map however you like.

WORLD

EUROPE

AFRICA

NORTH AMERICA

ATLANTIC OCEAN

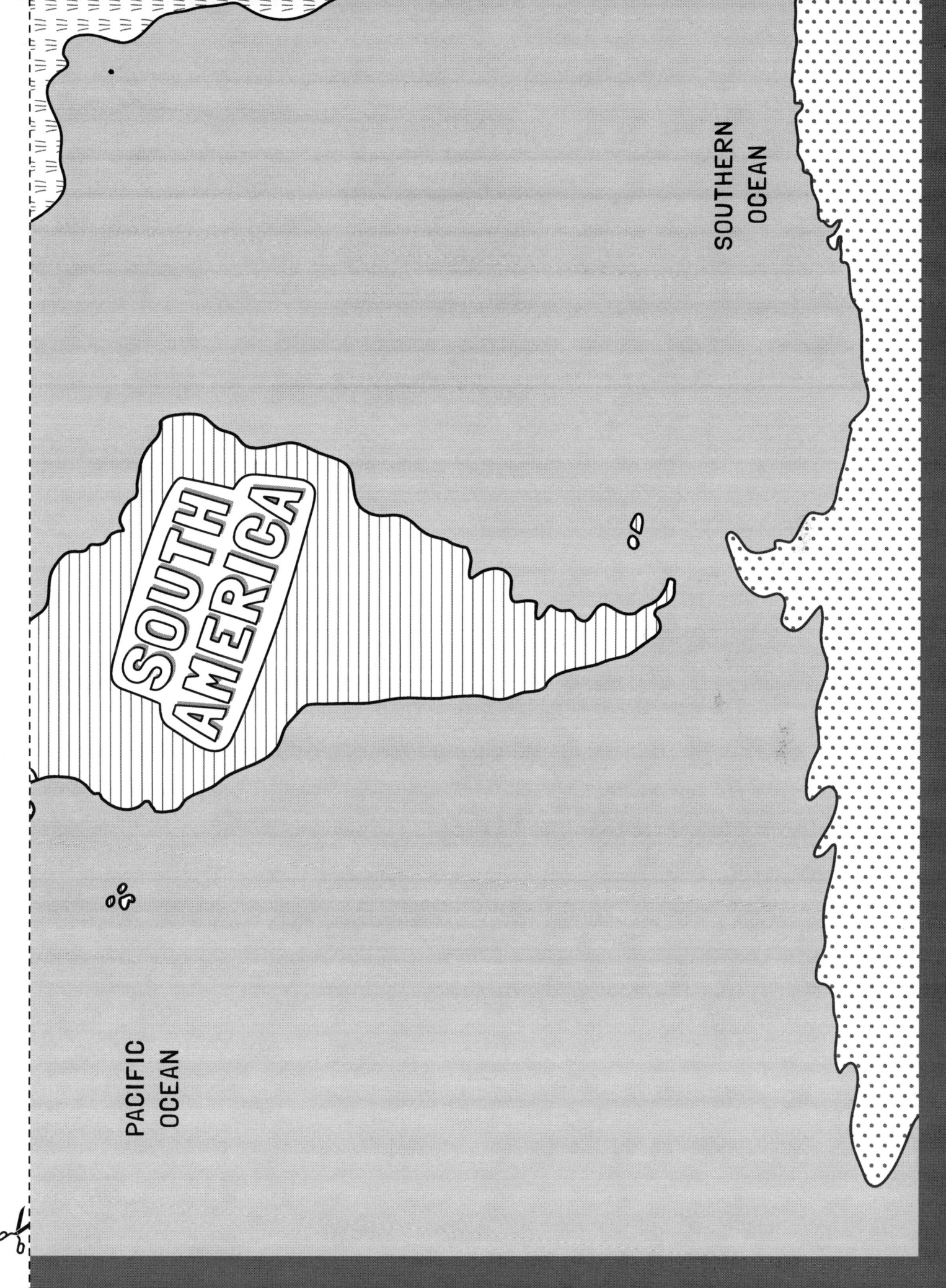

SOUTH
AMERICA

PACIFIC
OCEAN

SOUTHERN
OCEAN

MAP

ARCTIC
OCEAN

PACIFIC
OCEAN

ASIA

CUT & GLUE

STEP 1 Color the items on this page.

STEP 2 Cut them out.

STEP 3 Glue them onto the map.

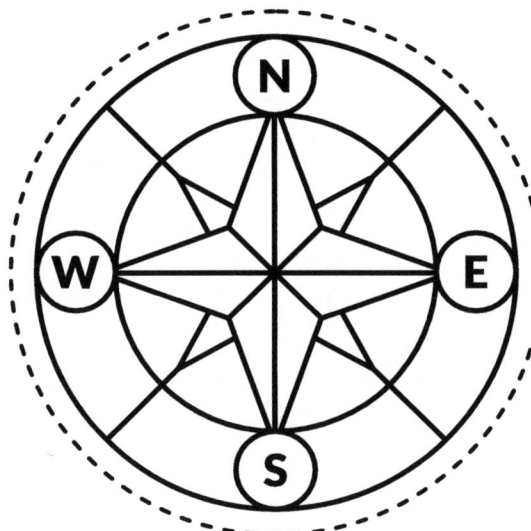

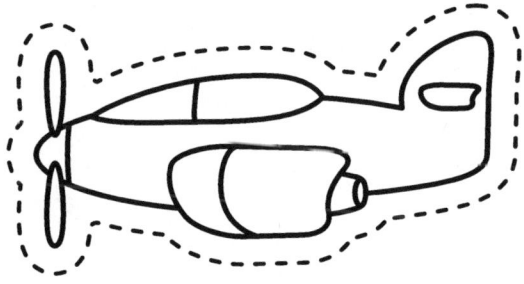

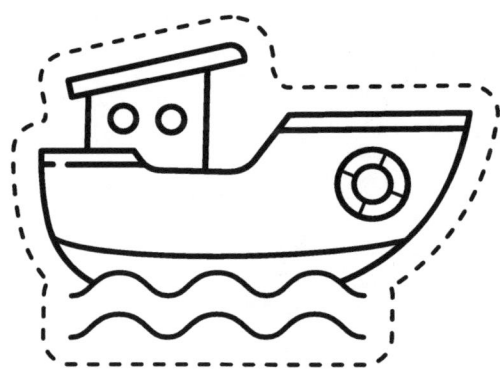

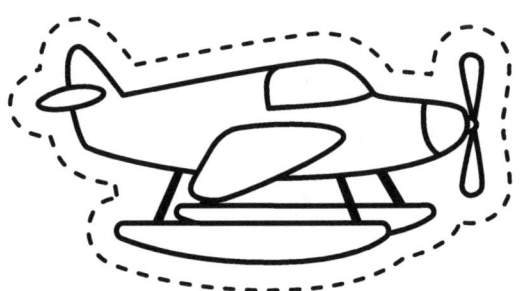

117

CUT & GLUE

STEP 1   Color the items on this page.

STEP 2   Cut them out.

STEP 3   Glue them onto the map.

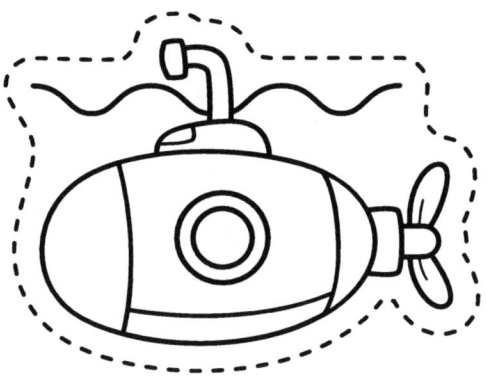
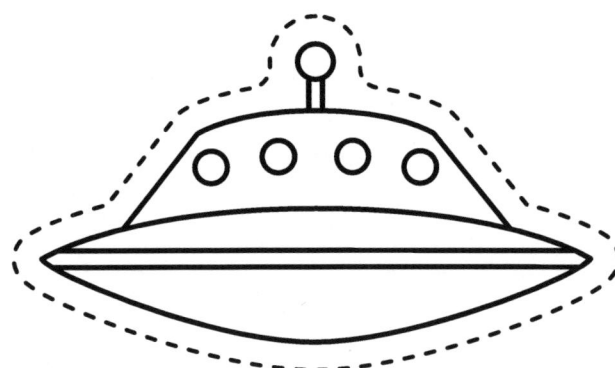

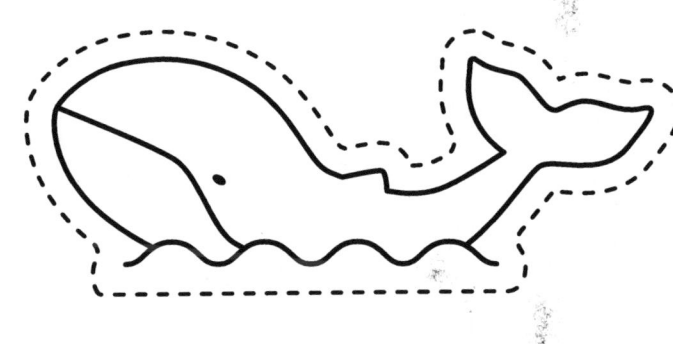

CODE BREAKER

Write all your answers from the marked puzzles in this book to answer the question.

Which of the world's continents is the biggest?

Page 48

Page 20

Page 36

Page 104

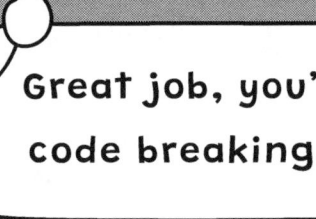

Great job, you're now a code breaking master!

SOLUTIONS

Let's take a trip around
OUR BIG, BEAUTIFUL WORLD

Our planet has...

$3+3+1=$

7

continents

PAGE 8

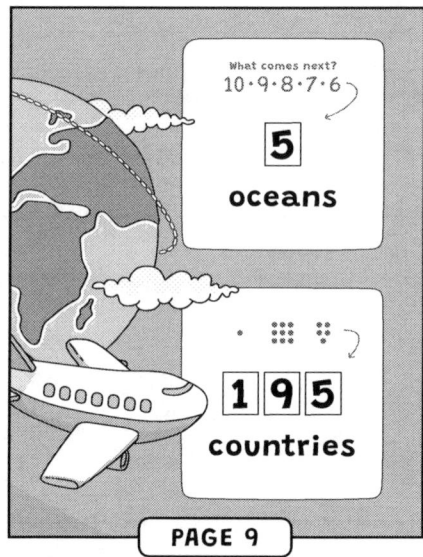

What comes next?
$10 \cdot 9 \cdot 8 \cdot 7 \cdot 6$

5
oceans

195
countries

PAGE 9

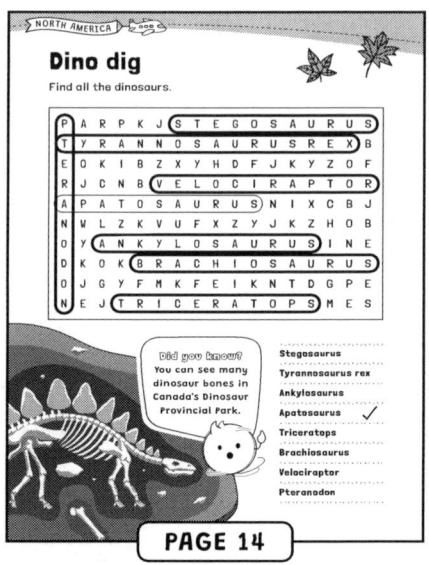

NORTH AMERICA
Dino dig
Find all the dinosaurs.

P	A	R	P	K	J	S	T	E	G	O	S	A	U	R	U	S
T	Y	R	A	N	N	O	S	A	U	R	U	S	R	E	X	B
E	O	K	I	B	Z	X	Y	H	D	F	J	K	Y	Z	O	F
R	J	C	N	B	V	E	L	O	C	I	R	A	P	T	O	R
A	P	A	T	O	S	A	U	R	U	S	N	I	X	C	B	J
N	W	L	Z	K	V	U	F	X	Z	Y	J	K	Z	H	O	B
O	Y	A	N	K	Y	L	O	S	A	U	R	U	S	I	N	E
D	K	O	K	B	R	A	C	H	I	O	S	A	U	R	U	S
O	J	G	Y	F	M	K	F	E	I	K	N	T	D	G	P	E
N	E	J	T	R	I	C	E	R	A	T	O	P	S	M	E	S

Did you know?
You can see many dinosaur bones in Canada's Dinosaur Provincial Park.

Stegosaurus
Tyrannosaurus rex
Ankylosaurus
Apatosaurus ✓
Triceratops
Brachiosaurus
Velociraptor
Pteranodon

PAGE 14

NORTH AMERICA
Beach beats
Let's write a reggae song!

Did you know?
Reggae music was invented in Jamaica.

Party time

It's party time
Let's have some **fun**

Playing our music
In the **sun**

We're going to dance
Till the day is **done**

Mama has cake
And gifts to be **won**

Are you ready now?
Three, two, **one** !

done   won
one   fun   sun

Add this word to the CODE BREAKER on page 121.

PAGE 20

SOUTH AMERICA
Keeping score
Which is the best player on the Brazilian team?
Add up the numbers to find out.

Pedro

STRENGTH	9
SPEED	7
GOALS	3 +
	19

Gabriel

STRENGTH	8
SPEED	5
GOALS	2 +
	15

Clara

STRENGTH	6
SPEED	9
GOALS	1 +
	16

SOCCER ? FOOTBALL

Did you know?
It's called **soccer** in the USA, Canada, and Australia, but in many countries, like Brazil, the game is called **football**.

PAGE 24

Help Callie the caiman find her way down the Amazon river to her favorite rock.

PAGE 27

SOUTH AMERICA
Let's go tango!
Complete the crossword puzzle of dancing styles.

m e r e n g u e
r u m b a — b o l e r o
c h a c h a
s a l s a
s a m b a — m a m b o
t a n g o

Did you know?
Tango is a ballroom dance that was invented in Argentina.

rumba ✓	tango
samba	cha cha
mambo	bolero
salsa	merengue

PAGE 28

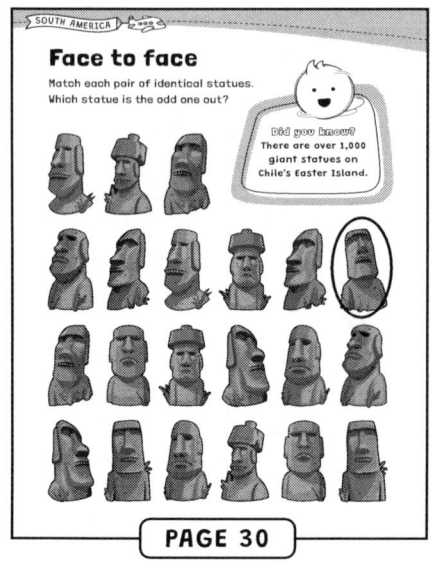

SOUTH AMERICA
Face to face
Match each pair of identical statues.
Which statue is the odd one out?

Did you know?
There are over 1,000 giant statues on Chile's Easter Island.

PAGE 30

SOLUTIONS

Spotlight on numbers

Put the numbers in the correct order

2 5 10 12 16
4 8 14 22 28
11 26 31 45 54 63
7 23 44 56 82 116
9 38 60 73 101 120

Did you know? Because it's on the tip of the continent, South Africa has many lighthouses to guide ships at night.

PAGE 34

Island adventure

Fill in the blanks to complete the story.

Last **summer**, I traveled with my **family** to Madagascar. It was so beautiful.

On the first day, we swam in the **ocean** and built a sandcastle.

On the second day, I saw a lemur! He had a long **tail** with black and white **stripes**.

On the third **day**, we sailed in a **boat** around the island.

It was the best **vacation** ever.

day
tail
boat
ocean
family
stripes
summer
vacation

Add this word to the CODE BREAKER on page 121.

PAGE 36

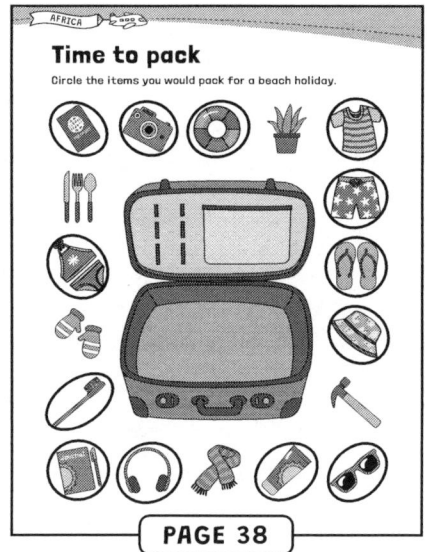

Time to pack

Circle the items you would pack for a beach holiday.

PAGE 38

Spot me

Add the correct stripes or spots to the animals.

Did you know? The cheetah is the world's fastest land animal.

Giraffe Zebra Cheetah Tiger

PAGE 40

Mindful Me: The good traveler

Zazzy is always respectful when visiting new countries.

How can we be better travelers?

Reading about the destination ☑YES ☐NO

Learning new words ☑YES ☐NO

Respecting different cultures ☑YES ☐NO

Littering ☐YES ☑NO

Making fun of people ☐YES ☑NO

PAGE 42

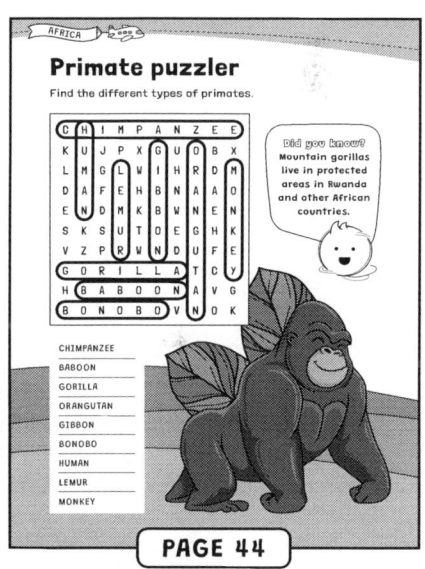

Primate puzzler

Find the different types of primates.

Did you know? Mountain gorillas live in protected areas in Rwanda and other African countries.

CHIMPANZEE
BABOON
GORILLA
ORANGUTAN
GIBBON
BONOBO
HUMAN
LEMUR
MONKEY

PAGE 44

Fantastic fabric

Fill in the empty boxes to complete the Nigerian pattern.

Did you know? Every country has its own traditional colors and patterns.

PAGE 46

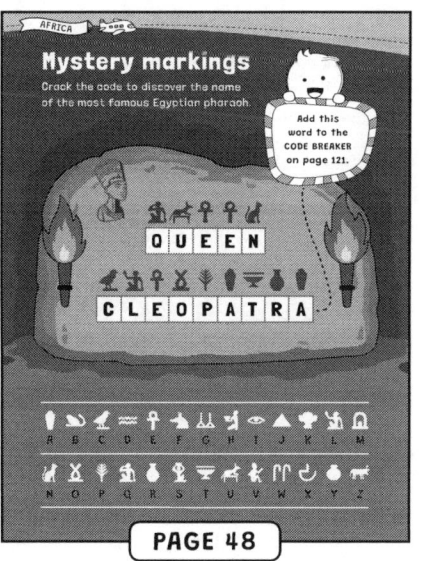

Mystery markings

Crack the code to discover the name of the most famous Egyptian pharaoh.

Add this word to the CODE BREAKER on page 121.

QUEEN

CLEOPATRA

A B C D E F G H I J K L M
N O P Q R S T U V W X Y Z

PAGE 48

SOLUTIONS

Find the fox

Can you spot 10 fennec foxes in the Moroccan town?

Did you know? The fennec fox is smaller than a cat and uses its long ears to keep cool in the desert.

PAGE 50

Being present

Four people came to the Flamenco show. Which one is being present?

PAGE 54

Seeing double

Find 11 differences between the real Mona Lisa and the fake.

Did you know? The Italian painter and inventor Leonardo da Vinci wrote backwards to keep his notes secret.

PAGE 58

Go team!

Who will win the top medals at the Olympics? Add up the scores to find out.

Did you know? The Olympic games started in Greece over 2,000 years ago.

2nd USA   1st Greece   3rd China

Team China
41
+ 38
79

Team Greece
45
+ 37
82

Team USA
36
+ 44
80

PAGE 60

Maestro of melody

Fill in the opposite of each word to reveal the answer to Zazzy's question.

DOWN → U P
OUT → I N
HAPPY → S A D
OVER → U N D E R
BOTTOM → T O P

Ludwig van Beethoven is a famous German musician. Which instrument did he play?

Violin   Cello   Piano   Guitar

PAGE 62

Writer's delight

Fill in the rhyming words to complete the poem.

book · way · me · find · there

My book

Come and have a look
I'm writing a **book**

I have so much to say
In a very special **way**

I see words everywhere
Stories here, stories **there**

I see them in my mind
Imagine things I will **find**

I write what I see
About you and about **me**

Did you know? The famous English writer Jane Austen never signed her name on her books.

PAGE 64

Sea escape

Help Marty the mouse get to the top of the Viking ship.

Did you know? Thursday is named after the Viking god, Thor!

1 2 3 4

PAGE 66

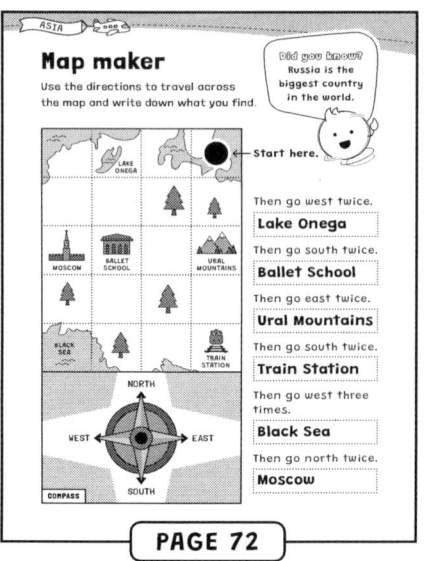

Map maker

Use the directions to travel across the map and write down what you find.

Did you know? Russia is the biggest country in the world.

Start here.

Then go west twice.
Lake Onega

Then go south twice.
Ballet School

Then go east twice.
Ural Mountains

Then go south twice.
Train Station

Then go west three times.
Black Sea

Then go north twice.
Moscow

NORTH · WEST · EAST · SOUTH · COMPASS

PAGE 72

SOLUTIONS

Ancient treasure

Millions of people visit the Treasury in Petra, Jordan. Spot the 10 differences between the left and right side.

PAGE 76

Record breaker

How tall is the Burj Khalifa? Add up the numbers to learn the answer.

```
  865
  454
  457
  439
+ 502
-------
2,717  feet
```

Did you know?
Burj Khalifa is the tallest building in the world. It has more than 160 floors!

PAGE 78

Chess challenge

Use the chessboard grid to fill in the blanks.

The **game** of **chess** was invented in **India**.
   C4   G2   F7

A chess **champion** is called a grandmaster.
          H3

The youngest grandmaster in the **world**
                                    A6
is **twelve** years old!
     D1

PAGE 80

Match the endangered animals to their names.

- Lemur
- Gorilla
- Elephant
- Rhinoceros
- Tiger
- Sea turtle
- Koala
- Whale
- Orangutan

PAGE 83

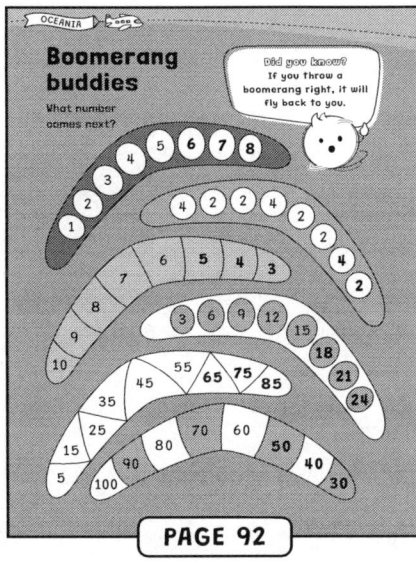

Boomerang buddies

What number comes next?

Did you know?
If you throw a boomerang right, it will fly back to you.

PAGE 92

Smart Dot
good for the planet, good for me

Zazzy is careful not to harm the coral reef or any creature that lives there.

Cool coral reef

In the picture on the next page, count the creatures that live in the coral reef.

- **21** Corals
- **2** Sea urchins
- **5** Starfish
- **7** Fish
- **2** Oysters
- **5** Seahorses
- **2** Stingrays
- **3** Jellyfish
- **2** Octopuses

PAGE 94

Village visit

Kai and Kuri are on their way to the beach to go fishing. Help them find their way through the Maori village.

PAGE 96

How many of the world's continents begin with the letter A? **4**

PAGE 101

SOLUTIONS

Look who's chilling

Scientists have arrived by submarine to study Antarctica. Check off all the animals they see.

☑ Petrel	☑ Icefish
☒ Tern	☑ Krill
☑ Albatross	☒ Starfish
☑ Whale	☑ Penguin
☑ Orca	☒ Gull
☑ Dolphin	☑ Seal
☒ Squid	☑ Sea lion

PAGE 102

Photo album

Fill in the names of the countries in the photographs.

Kenya — Spain — Jordan — Mexico — Japan — Brazil

Add this word to the CODE BREAKER on page 121.

PAGE 104

Souvenir sorter

Match the country stickers to the correct continents.

FRANCE — UNITED STATES OF AMERICA — AUSTRALIA — United Arab Emirates — CHILE — EGYPT

North America / South America / Africa / Europe / Asia / Australia & Oceania / Antarctica

PAGE 105

Magnet mix-up

Unscramble the magnet letters to reveal six countries.

ADCANA — CANADA
INEGAIR — NIGERIA
TAIYL — ITALY
URTYEK — TURKEY
HICAN — CHINA
IFIJ — FIJI

PAGE 106

CODE BREAKER

Write all your answers from the marked puzzles in this book to answer the question.

Which of the world's continents is the biggest?

Page 48	C L E O P A T R A
Page 20	S U N
Page 36	V A C A T I O N
Page 104	J A P A N

Great job, you're now a code breaking master!

PAGE 121

Find more activity books and free downloads at
wewonderpress.com

If you enjoyed this book, please consider leaving us a review. We appreciate every single one, and it allows us to reach more people.

Made in the USA
Monee, IL
10 July 2025

20927311R00070